7/09

20

Artists   -90145

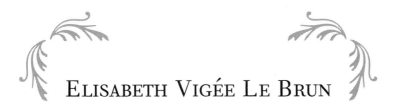

ELISABETH VIGÉE LE BRUN

Elisabeth Vigée Le Brun

The Odyssey
of an Artist
in an Age
of Revolution

GITA MAY

Yale University Press
New Haven and London

Published with assistance from the Annie Burr Lewis Fund.

Designed by Mary Valencia
Set in Monotype Fournier type by Duke & Company, Devon, Pennsylvania
Printed in the United States of America by Edwards Brothers, Ann Arbor, Michigan

Library of Congress Cataloging-in-Publication Data
May, Gita.
Elisabeth Vigée Le Brun : the odyssey of an artist in an age of revolution /
Gita May.
p.   cm.
Includes bibliographical references and index.
ISBN 0-300-10872-9 (hardcover : alk. paper)
1. Vigée Le Brun, Elisabeth Louise, 1755–1842. 2. Portrait painters—France—
Biography. I. Vigée Le Brun, Elisabeth Louise, 1755–1842. II. Title.
ND553.V5325M39 2005
759.4—dc22
                                                        2005004788

A catalogue record for this book is available from the British Library.

The paper in this book meets the guidelines for permanence and durability of
the Committee on Production Guidelines for Book Longevity of the Council on
Library Resources.

10 9 8 7 6 5 4 3 2 1

For Irving May, always

CONTENTS

ELISABETH VIGÉE LE BRUN

❧ *Introduction* ❧

THE NAME OF ELISABETH VIGÉE LE BRUN (1755–1842), whose remarkably long lifetime spanned the last decades of the Old Regime, the Revolution, the Empire, the Restoration, and the July Monarchy, is familiar enough, primarily because of what has been characterized by Ann Sutherland Harris and Linda Nochlin in *Women Artists, 1550–1950*, as her prodigious talent" and as the much sought-after portraitist of not only European royalty and nobility, but also of notable personalities in the arts and letters of her time.[1]

Among Vigée Le Brun's best-known works are her famous portraits of Marie-Antoinette, either alone or surrounded by her children, and her more intimate and informal self-portraits, either before her easel with palette in hand, or in her role as mother in an appealingly tender and protective pose with her young daughter, Julie. Even mistresses, royal and otherwise, sat for her, as her delightful portraits of the ill-fated Madame du Barry and of Lady Hamilton testify. And there are her striking portraits of Hubert Robert and Joseph Vernet, the renowned artists who encouraged her efforts as a young painter, and of the celebrated but controversial Germaine de Staël (in the guise of her famous heroine Corinne), whose circle at Coppet, on Lake Geneva, she visited in 1808.

Germaine Greer, in *The Obstacle Race: The Fortunes of Women Painters and Their Work*, describes Vigée Le Brun's distinctive talent as a painter accurately if somewhat condescendingly: "Her genius was all communication and sociability, and portrait-painting her métier."[2] What has been overlooked is that Vigée Le Brun deserves her place alongside such great eighteenth-century artists as Fragonard, Boucher, Chardin, and Greuze, rather than as a merely successful portraitist in her own time because of her uncanny ability to please and flatter the many individuals, and especially the women of high rank, who posed for their likeness.[3]

Edgar Munhall, Curator Emeritus of the Frick Collection in New York, upon viewing a 1982 exhibition of Vigée Le Brun's works at the Kimbell Art Museum in Fort Worth, was so impressed that he wrote in the *New York Times* that it was well worth the trip to Texas and that "the resulting assemblage of fifty-seven paintings, drawings and documents is one of the most seductive, intelligent and moving monograph exhibitions seen in many years: it is the revelation of genius."[4]

Vigée Le Brun's immensely seductive appeal as a portraitist was due to a highly individual style she developed early on in her astonishingly successful career. It is marked by a sensuous, brilliant, and creamy coloristic use of pigments, reminiscent of Rubens and especially of Van Dyck at their most informal and spontaneous. The subjects of her portraits are generally represented in natural, relaxed, informal, intimate attitudes, facing the beholder with a calm, self-absorbed, reflective gaze. There are discreet, gentle hints at antiquity, notably in the manner in which the artist posed her sitters and draped them in light, free-flowing costumes. If the classical influence is clear in the pose and attributes of many of Vigée Le Brun's paintings, it is subtly transformed by a flowing grace, a smooth elegance evocative of Boucher and Fragonard. At the same time, a pre-Romantic mood also pervades her portraits, frequently evident in backgrounds consisting of landscapes with dramatic, cloud-streaked skies, and mountains as well as waterfalls. This eclectic combination of neoclassicism and pre-Romanticism should not surprise us, for we find it prevalent everywhere in the latter half of the eighteenth century.

Vigée Le Brun was keenly aware of the new spirit that pervaded the arts and letters, and her portraits reflect a Rousseauan ideal of femininity made of modesty, gentleness, and vulnerability. Her self-portraits with her daughter, showing her locked with the child in a tender, loving embrace, and her famous representation of Marie-Antoinette, not as a haughty, autocratic monarch, but as a devoted mother and dignified matron, are clear ideological statements. The queen and her entourage must have sensed that such portraiture could help to repair her badly damaged image as scandalously promiscuous and profligate. No wonder, therefore, that Marie-Antoinette consistently treated Vigée Le Brun with the utmost kindness and consideration.

Ironically, the artist who would be condemned by the revolutionaries for her close association with the monarchy and nobility of the Old Regime actually owed a great deal of her early and spectacular success to her uncanny ability of representing her aristocratic subjects as unpretentious, thoughtful people in informal attire caught in moments of unguarded introspection.

Until quite recently, art historians and critics have given Vigée Le Brun only grudging recognition as the epitome of the Old Regime court portraitist whose fashionable style embodied sentimentalized neoclassicism with a flattering idealization of her royal or titled subjects. That she was a woman artist doubtless contributed to this underappreciation. For instance, Michael Levey presents this superficial, condescending, and subtly hostile assessment in *Rococo to Revolution:* "Naturalness, which was not at all a discovery of Rousseau's but which he had made into a doctrine, was really the century's last burst of optimism. At the emotional extreme it found Madame Vigée Le Brun, who gave it *chic*, and confused simplicity with goodness of heart. Ravished by the charm of her own appearance, and hardly able to paint a male sitter, Vigée Le Brun continued the century's cult of women."[5] Even such a leading feminist as Simone de Beauvoir saw in Vigée Le Brun primarily a narcissistic painter who never wearied of putting her own self or "her smiling maternity on her canvases."[6]

Vigée Le Brun's overdue reemergence in the limelight is attested to by a lively and enthusiastic article by Wendy Wasserstein, the Pulitzer prize–winning playwright, which paid the artist this witty tribute: "She was a self-supporting artist, a woman of the world, who managed against all political odds to continue her career. Looking at her extensive work, and the consistent quality of it, one begins to discard any notion that her success was due to being charming or witty or well connected. Madame Le Brun was serious and very good. And though I'm sure she was the best of friends with the kings and queens of Poland, Russia, and France, my hunch is they let her stay for more than tea because ultimately they too recognized that she was serious and very good."[7]

Women like Vigée Le Brun who achieved renown could not but be acutely aware that they challenged the conventional notion of womanhood as one of dependence and vulnerability. Hence their efforts to reconcile—or at least to explore—the uneasy, sometimes conflicting relation between their public and personal identities: the often controversial image they projected to the outer world, and their private version of the self. Novels, autobiographies, and letters deal with this problematic relationship.[8]

That the literary genres favored by notable eighteenth-century women should be the novel, the memoir, and the letter is no mere coincidence. For obvious reasons women felt more at ease in literary forms that had not been rigidly codified by the officially sanctioned classical canons that left ample room for spontaneity, intimacy, and informality, and that allowed them to delve into the world of introspection and imagination without undue concern for accepted rules and conventions.

No wonder, therefore, that the aging Vigée Le Brun should have yielded to the urgings of her friends as well as to a strong inner need to recount her life's rich experience in her autobiography, unpretentiously titled *Souvenirs*, first published in a three-volume edition in 1835.[9] As she informed those of her loyal friends who had urged her to record for posterity the events of an exceptionally long and productive life, she found that setting down these recollections in an informal style that a woman would resort to in writing to an intimate friend would best suit her needs. As an artist rather than writer, Vigée Le Brun felt especially inhibited about the idea of attempting to express her thoughts and feelings with the pen rather than the brush. Writing to a woman friend rather than to some vague, abstract reading public helped her overcome her initial hesitations over the whole project.

Souvenirs affords enticing but incomplete insights into the vicissitudes and victories of Vigée Le Brun as a self-supporting woman artist at a time when such a career had very few precedents. The fact that she seemingly speaks with candor, clarity, and transparency does not automatically open the door to her inner psyche. Paradoxically, Vigée Le Brun's rhetoric as an autobiographer owes a great deal to Rousseau, whom she greatly admired in spite of her abiding loyalty to the Royalist cause.

Yet as a woman, Vigée Le Brun strongly felt that she did not owe it to her reader to bare her soul and "tell all." For her a personal memoir need not be confessional. One would seek in vain in her *Souvenirs* the tortured quest for self-identity, the haunting feelings of guilt and remorse characteristic of Rousseau's *Confessions*. Vigée Le Brun's literary sensibility is more neoclassical than pre-Romantic and was further nurtured by her aristocratic friends and protectors and by those writers, poets, and dramatists who frequented the same conservative circles and whom she hosted in her own salon: a rather fastidious sense of what is acceptable both in life and art, a keen admiration for those qualities of intellect and reason demonstrated through wit and humor, and a need to veil the deepest and most hurtful thoughts and feelings behind an attitude of breezy lightheartedness and steadfast optimism.

Probably also for reasons of feminine *pudeur* (inadequately rendered in English as "modesty"), Vigée Le Brun, unlike Rousseau, refrained from dwelling on the most intimate, painful, or humiliating aspects of her life and career, preferring to underscore her triumphs and accomplishments. And unlike Rousseau, she would not turn her autobiography into a personal apology paradoxically replete with demeaning self-accusations. There are many significant gaps in Vigée Le Brun's *Souvenirs*, and her own highly subjective and selective interpretation of events needs to be probed in order to gain a fuller understanding of her life and career in the context of her tumultuous times.

I hope that this book will not only contribute significantly to the renewal of interest in Vigée Le Brun, but also present a full-length portrait of a woman artist who managed to achieve greatness in spite of numerous obstacles due to her gender and to the explosive political times in which she lived. No great artist springs out of a vacuum. I will therefore endeavor to re-create the exciting and vital cultural climate that surrounded the young and ambitious Elisabeth Louise Vigée learning her craft in her father's studio and coming into personal contact with some of the most notable French artists of the latter part of the eighteenth century, Hubert Robert, Joseph Vernet, and Jean-Baptiste Greuze, among others. Her personal acquaintanceship and even familiarity with monarchs, aristocrats, writers, and artists, as well as her unusually long life span, extraordinary career, and nomadic existence, should afford an exceptionally broad panorama of the European political and cultural scene at an especially swift-changing juncture of its history.

CHAPTER ONE

❧ *Early Years* ❧

ON APRIL 16, 1755, during the reign of Louis XV, a baby girl was born to
Louis Vigée, a minor but well-connected Parisian portraitist, and Jeanne
Maissin, a handsome and pious hairdresser, daughter of a *marchand-
laboureur,* or merchant farmer, who hailed from Rossart, in the province
of Luxembourg. The couple, who had married in 1750, lived on the
bustling right bank rue Coquilière, still in existence today, and the infant was baptized in the nearby imposing Church of Saint Eustache,
in the Halles Quarter, which provided the capital with all its essential
foodstuff and which Emile Zola would call the belly of Paris. (In 1969
the neighborhood lost much of its animated street scenes and a variety
of colors and smells when the great market was moved to the Parisian
southern suburb of Rungis.)

The infant was named Elisabeth-Louise. She was the couple's
firstborn, and three years later, on December 2, 1758, another child followed, a boy named Louis-Jean-Baptiste-Etienne. Etienne was a beautiful, bright child and the object of his mother's affections. He would
eventually become a fairly successful poet and playwright. Perhaps the
most notable feature about him is that he managed to further his career
through all the political upheavals of his time and prospered under the

Old Regime, the Revolution, and the Empire. A delightfully lively portrait of him as a schoolboy, probably painted by his sister as early as 1773, is now part of the collection of the Saint Louis Art Museum (plate 1).

Elisabeth did not have her younger brother's winning personality. A rather awkward, skinny, and ungainly child who tended to stoop because she had grown too fast, and with pale, drawn facial features, she was painfully aware of her mother's preference for her brother, whose youthful wrongdoings were easily forgiven, while she benefited from no such indulgence. Vigée Le Brun readily acknowledges in her autobiography that, at this time of her life, "I was ugly" (I, 29), an admission she could make without too much rancor, since she was to grow into an exceptionally lovely woman whose good looks would play a not insignificant part in furthering her brilliant career as a court painter. But as a little girl she could not help but observe helplessly that "all my imperfections distressed my mother" (I, 29).

Fortunately for her self-esteem, young Elisabeth had a special hold on her father, who consistently showed her great tenderness and, perhaps even more importantly, strong support for her budding artistic talent. Primarily a portraitist and pastellist, Louis Vigée (1715–1767) did not achieve the kind of fame associated with such leading painters as François Boucher, Jean-Honoré Fragonard, Jean-Baptiste Greuze, and Jean-Siméon Chardin, but he gained sufficient recognition to become a member and professor at the Academy of Saint Luc, a respectable if considerably less prestigious, conservative, and selective institution than the Académie Royale de Peinture et de Sculpture.

Louis Vigée was not only a skillful and competent painter; he doubtless also had ambition and possessed a winning personality, for he succeeded in gaining the goodwill and even friendship of some of the most influential artists of his day, notably Greuze. In her *Souvenirs* Vigée Le Brun even boasts about the fact that her father hosted and attended dinners comprising not only distinguished artists, but notable men of letters as well (I, 26). She would indeed owe a great deal to her father's connections in the world of artists, especially in the early crucial stages of her career.

Although Louis Vigée, as primarily a portraitist and pastellist, practiced what was then considered a relatively secondary genre in the official, academic hierarchy—which placed history painting at the top of the ladder and downgraded landscape, still life, and portraiture, because in the official view these required neither imagination nor erudition—he was able to obtain some official commissions. Thus he was invited on behalf of King Louis XV to contribute two paintings on "a gallant" theme for the 1764 exhibit of the Academy of Saint Luc.[1] In such paintings, now unfortunately no longer extant, Louis Vigée must have endeavored to emulate the delightfully seductive and slyly erotic compositions and pastorals popularized by Boucher and Fragonard, masters of the fashionable rococo style, which epitomized a libertine and pleasure-loving ideal of art as escape into a world of perpetual youth and sexual gratification without guilt.

The French political and cultural climate was undergoing momentous changes in the early 1750s. A profound transformation in political and social ideas was taking place, and public opinion began to play a crucial role in politics and society. Manifestations of the growing malaise became more marked, and subjects long regarded as untouchable became matters for critical inquiry and comment. In 1749 Denis Diderot's controversial and provocative *Letter on the Blind*, which posited a cosmology of the universe based on matter and chance, earned him a three-month imprisonment in the medieval fortress of Vincennes on the eastern outskirts of Paris. In 1750 Jean-Jacques Rousseau published his explosive *Discourse on the Sciences and Arts*, and his even more radical *Discourse on the Origin of Inequality* appeared in 1755. In both works Rousseau posited that the development of the arts, the progressive refinement in manners, mores, and standards of beauty and taste, and the impressive advances and achievements in architecture, theater, opera, literature, and painting had not been matched by social and ethical progress and only testified to an ever-widening rift between nature and culture as well as to the increasing degeneration of social and moral values. In 1754 Pierre-Louis de Maupertuis, the noted mathematician and astronomer, published his *Essay on the Formation of Organized Bodies*, in which, for the first time, the idea of evolution of the species is stated in philosophical terms. The publication of Voltaire's *Essay on the Manners and Spirit of Nations* in 1756 confirmed his reputation as creator of a new genre, the philosophy of history.

In 1755, the year of Vigée Le Brun's birth, Louis XV, who had mounted the throne in 1723, was still a handsome and popular monarch, although his general indifference to affairs of state was beginning to affect both foreign affairs and domestic policy. Perhaps some beneficial influence that filled the political vacuum at this time was filled by Madame de Pompadour, the king's mistress and confidante until her death in 1764. Of middle-class origin, she was a woman of intelligence and culture who patronized such controversial writers as Voltaire and encouraged such artists as Boucher and Fragonard.[2]

As was then the custom with infants of the bourgeoisie, which in this and many other respects aped the mores of the aristocracy, shortly after her birth Elisabeth was entrusted to the care of a wet nurse who was a peasant woman in the village of Epernon, near Chartres. Elisabeth spent the first five years of her life in the farmhouse of her wet nurse. Such treatment of a young child may seem callous by today's standards, but it was common practice under the Old Regime.[3] The practice of sending infants to some farm in the country, leaving it to a peasant woman to act as wet nurse and surrogate mother, continued even long after the publication of Rousseau's *Emile* in 1762, which was to revolutionize the concept of early childhood by underscoring its vital importance in the physical, psychological, and moral development of the individual. That the custom of wet nursing survived well into the nineteenth century, despite Rousseau's admonitions against it, is attested to by the fact that in Gustave Flaubert's *Madame Bovary*, published in 1857, Emma Bovary's infant girl is placed for wet nursing with the wife of a local carpenter.

At the age of six Elisabeth was enrolled as a *pensionnaire* at the Convent of the Trinité, on the rue de Charonne, in the Faubourg Saint Antoine, where she remained until her eleventh birthday. This was by no means an unusual educational arrangement under the Old Regime. Young girls of the aristocracy and bourgeoisie were placed in convents where they would be expected to learn such rudimentary skills as reading, writing, counting, sewing, embroidering, as well as the proper rules of social behavior.

What Vigée Le Brun has to say about the years spent at the convent focuses on her precocious and irrepressible talent. She tells us that she drew and sketched tirelessly and on every available space. The margins of her schoolbooks and even those of her classmates were covered with drawings of heads, either full face or in profile. She even went so far as to cover the walls of the convent dormitory with charcoal figures and landscapes, a transgression for which she was duly punished (I, 24). Even during recess time she would trace on the sand whatever came through her head: "I remember that at the age of seven or eight, I drew by the lamp the head of a bearded man, which I have always kept. I showed it to my father who cried out with joy: 'You will be a painter, my child!'" (I, 24).

Vigée Le Brun's account of her early years reveals a powerful attachment for her father and a difficult, strained relationship with her mother. The tribute she pays her father's rather modest talent is indeed a touching one: "My father painted very well in pastel; there are even portraits by him that would be worthy of the famous La Tour" (I, 25), a reference to Maurice-Quentin de La Tour (1704–1788), probably the best French portraitist of the eighteenth century. Whatever Louis Vigée may have lacked in talent as a painter of the first magnitude he made up for with a sunny disposition, immense gregariousness, and great charm and wit. His personality seems to have been so irresistible that people would select him as their portraitist "in order to enjoy his delightful conversation" (I, 25).

Louis Vigée's passion for his art, if one is to take at face value the testimony of his loving daughter, was all-consuming and at times reached the point of comical distraction and forgetfulness. An example of this fanatical dedication, which made a great impression on his daughter, is related in *Souvenirs*. One day, when all dressed up in his best finery, including a wig and a waistcoat with gold braid and sword, he had a last minute inspiration, so he partially undressed to retouch a painting he had been working on, and then walked out of the house without troubling to put on the proper outfit (I, 25).

This charming man was not without all-too-human failings. He was an unabashed hedonist, and his love of the good things in life frequently went beyond the boundaries of propriety and common sense. While he worshipped his beautiful, pious wife and was dedicated to his children, especially to his precociously talented daughter, he had an irresistible weakness for women. By Vigée Le Brun's own admission "they turned his head," and on New Year's Day he would run around the streets of Paris solely in order to kiss all those he would meet "under the pretext of wishing them a Happy New Year" (I, 26).

Even Louis Vigée's premature death, on May 9, 1767 (at the age of fifty-two), was probably caused by his excessive devotion to sensual gratifications. He swallowed a fishbone, which lodged in his throat. Incisions performed by one of the leading surgeons of the day failed to relieve the patient, not surprising in view of the limited means of contemporary medicine. The wounds became infected, and after two months of awful suffering Vigée expired, leaving his family in tears and depriving his daughter of her most supportive guide and mentor. In *Souvenirs* Vigée Le Brun paints an arresting picture of her father on his deathbed taking his final leave of his children. The resulting tableau not only shows her own keen visual sensitivity, hardly surprising in a painter, but also a highly developed sense of pathos and melodrama worthy of Greuze, from whom she not only learned a great deal, but who would also play a key role in her career as loyal and steadfast supporter: "When he felt that his last moments were at hand, my father expressed the desire to see my brother and me. Sobbing, we both approached the bed. His features had cruelly deteriorated. His eyes, his physiognomy, always so animated, no longer had any movement, for the pallor and coldness of death had already taken hold of them. We seized his icy hand, covered it with our kisses, and bathed it with our tears. He made an effort and raised himself to give us his benediction: 'Be happy, my children,' he said. An hour later, our dear father was no more!" (I, 32).

In this touching scene we find all the essential elements characteristic of an aesthetic of vividly expressed emotionalism typical of the latter part of the eighteenth century, whether it be in the theater, the novel, or the visual arts. This is indeed a striking family scene that Diderot, Rousseau, or Greuze would not have disavowed. Whether it is strictly truthful or embellished and dramatized by memory is of course impossible to say. The more skeptical reader will be inclined to think that the aging memoirist took her cue from the writers and artists who had shaped her own sensibilities, notably from Rousseau's *Confessions*, a work with which she was thoroughly familiar, in order to endow this traumatic episode of her childhood with an aura of morality and dramatic intensity deemed appropriate for such a portentous event.

Her father's premature death left young Elisabeth in such a state of prostration that it took her a long time to pick up her brushes again. One of her father's colleagues and best friends, Gabriel-François Doyen, a highly respected history painter and member of the Académie frequently praised in Diderot's *Salons* for his dramatic flair and coloristic virtuosity, paid her frequent visits, exhorting her that work was the best remedy against life's misfortunes and urging her to return to her drawing and painting. And indeed Vigée Le Brun would always find her greatest solace in her work. Throughout the most trying circumstances of her life, practicing her craft with passionate and single-minded dedication would remain her best and most reliable refuge against adversity.

She began painting and drawing from nature around this time, doing several portraits in succession, both in oil and in pastel, and she struck up a friendship with another young aspiring woman painter, Rosalie Bocquet. Rosalie, also the daughter of an artist, was a talented portraitist, but unlike Elisabeth she would soon renounce her ambition, marry, and opt for domesticity. Because the Bocquets had some influence at court, Marie-Antoinette appointed the recently married Rosalie concierge at the Château de La Muette, a post that came with an assured income and various privileges. Yet Rosalie, unlike Elisabeth, refused to emigrate after the outbreak of the Revolution, and she would pay the ultimate price for her connection with the queen by being sent to the guillotine.

The two young girls took drawing lessons from Gabriel Briard, a history painter and academician of some note who rounded out his income by offering advice and criticism to young ladies. Briard had been commissioned to paint the Banquet Hall of the Versailles Palace and occupied a studio and living quarters at the Louvre, then home for certain privileged artists. Of course, Elisabeth and Rosalie could not attend Briard's regular classes, which were reserved for young men only.

If the Louvre was a welcome haven for aspiring art students, its surroundings were far from safe for young women. To avoid the dirt, congestion, and dangers of the streets, Elisabeth and Rosalie brought along food in baskets. Much later Vigée Le Brun wrote with some nostalgia that she "never ate anything as good" as those picnic-style meals with her friend (I, 33).

In the intervening years Elisabeth's gawky shape had pleasingly filled out, and her facial features had become strikingly alluring: "A metamorphosis had taken place in me, and I had become pretty" (I, 34). Elisabeth's handsome good looks developed as impressively as her talent as an artist. Most noteworthy, perhaps, is that she would use her personal beauty and charm most skillfully, both in her art, particularly in her self-portraits, and in her dealings with patrons at court and in high society, where youth and physical attractiveness were highly prized. At the same time, however, her exceptionally appealing feminine attributes would set a real obstacle in her path as a truly serious and original artist by making her vulnerable, especially in the early phase of her career, to all kinds of rumors and insinuations about the nature of her relations with some of her male patrons and sitters, and even about the authenticity and authorship of her paintings.

Elisabeth was making rapid progress, and her work was beginning to be noticed, for she had a natural talent and facility that needed only nurturing to blossom. Her early efforts were encouraged by Greuze, whose edifying compositions on bourgeois and rustic family themes and dramas met with immense enthusiasm on the part of the public and critics, notably Diderot in his *Salons*.[4] Greuze would remain a staunch friend and supporter of Vigée Le Brun, even after the Revolution would force her into exile, and he would be the first to greet her in person upon her belated return to France in 1802 (II, 102).

Another friendly guide and mentor was Hubert Robert, a painter whose unique talent was to blend Roman landscapes and architecture in picturesque and evocative compositions highlighting temples and other such ancient edifices in a melancholy state of ruins. One of Vigée Le Brun's most arresting portraits is that of this artist, painted in 1788 (plate 2). In *Souvenirs* Vigée Le Brun would accuse the great neoclassical master Jacques-Louis David of having contributed, in his revolutionary fanaticism during the Terror, to the arbitrary imprisonment and cruel treatment of Robert, among other artists (II, 250).[5]

Young Elisabeth also received very helpful advice and guidance from Joseph Vernet, who was noted for his landscapes and seascapes and who also happened to be one of Diderot's favorite painters. Like Nicolas Poussin in the seventeenth century, Vernet had opted to live and work in Italy over an extended period of time, but in 1753 he decided to return to France, whereupon he was commissioned by Louis XV to paint a series of the major ports of France. He gave Elisabeth the following advice: "My child, don't follow any academic system. Consult only the works of the great masters of Italy, as well as the Flemish ones; but above all work as much as you can from nature: nature is the first of our masters. If you study it carefully, it will prevent you from becoming mannered" (I, 34).

One of Vigée Le Brun's earliest portraits was that of Joseph Vernet, painted in 1778 (plate 3), and it is one of her most inspired, masterful, and striking representations of a male subject. Vernet is shown sitting, lightly leaning on a table. He is dressed in informal attire consisting of a gray coat with red collar, a yellow vest, and a white scarf loosely tied around his neck. He holds his palette and brushes in his left hand while lightly leaning on his right hand. He is wigless, and his thinning gray hair frames his still-youthful, eager, and animated face.

CHAPTER TWO

≫ *First Successes* ≪

WHILE ELISABETH and her friend Rosalie Bocquet went about their daily task of studying their craft in Briard's atelier, they were hardly aware of the major political and social events as well as the scandals that rocked the monarchy. In 1768 Marie Lesczynska, daughter of Stanislas I of Poland, queen of France and royal consort of Louis XV, who had borne his ten children but had led a retired existence at court and had made no attempt to rival the king's mistresses, died. The king's grief was of short duration, and he hastened to acknowledge his new mistress, Jeanne Bécu, a beautiful courtesan of illegitimate birth and mistress of Count Jean du Barry. She was nominally married to her lover's brother, Guillaume, and was installed at court in 1769 as Countess du Barry.

One of the king's first gifts to his new favorite was a château and surrounding park at Louveciennes, where Elisabeth would later make her acquaintance as her portraitist. Unlike her predecessor, Madame de Pompadour, an intelligent and cultured woman who even tended to be sympathetic to the Encyclopedists. Madame du Barry was a rather vacuous and mannered coquette intent above all to retain her good looks and to hold onto the king.

Within a few months after her husband's death, on May 9, 1767, Elisabeth's mother remarried. Her new spouse, Jean-François Le Sèvre, was a jeweler with an elegant shop situated on the rue Saint-Honoré. This move to a fashionable section of Paris facilitated Elisabeth's eventual social rise accompanying her first artistic successes. Yet she nurtured great animosity toward her stepfather and had a hard time overcoming her grief over her loss of her father. Her mother tried her best to comfort Elisabeth by taking her to view paintings both in public and private exhibitions, a well-meaning gesture that was not especially appreciated: "Seeing me so affected by the cruel loss I had incurred, my mother could think of nothing better than taking me to look at pictures" (I, 35).

In her autobiography Vigée Le Brun proudly stresses the fact that she was essentially a self-taught artist. And indeed, as a woman, she was precluded from enrolling in the official curriculum of the Académie, and therefore had to fall back on taking drawing lessons from Briard, the history painter. But her singular talent, especially as a portraitist, manifested itself early. Immediate family members sat for these early portraits, especially her mother and younger brother, Etienne. One of these likenesses of Etienne was dated 1773, when Elisabeth was in her early teens.

The portrait of Etienne (see plate 1) is a striking example of Vigée Le Brun's prodigious and precocious talent, especially at capturing a personality in an unselfconscious moment of introspection and self-revelation. Young Etienne is pictured holding a portfolio under his left arm and a pen in his right hand and is gazing at us with an animated and assured yet self-contained smile. He is caught in an unguarded but revealing moment: he appears as the incarnation of youthful optimism and belief in his future accomplishments.

This spirited youthful work has a delightfully seductive quality of freshness, intimacy, and spontaneity clearly foreshadowing Vigée

Le Brun's later virtuosity as a master portraitist. At the same time, the sitter's obvious charm and good looks make clear why he was his mother's favorite. With her generous nature Vigée Le Brun held no grudge against her brother. She took pride in his handsome good looks, wit, and literary talents, and she made every effort to further his career as poet and author of comedies through her own growing influence as a successful artist. His poetry was published in such influential journals as the *Journal de Paris* and the *Almanach des Muses*, of which he became editor in 1789. He also wrote comedies in the style of Marivaux, notably *Les Aveux difficiles* (first staged in 1783) and *L'Entrevue* (first performed in 1788). Both plays were performed at the Comédie Française.[1]

Elisabeth also promoted Etienne's social advancement. In 1784 he made a brilliant move with his marriage to Suzanne-Marie-Françoise Rivière, the third of seven children born to Jean-Baptiste Rivière and his wife, Catherine-Antoinette Foulquier. The Rivière family, of French origin, was attached to the courts of Saxony, and the bride's father occupied the post of *chargé d'affaires* in Paris of the Elector of Saxony, a post he occupied for nearly five decades.

Suzanne Vigée was a charming and gifted young woman with an expressive face and large, affectionate brown eyes, all of which is evident in the wonderfully vibrant portrait painted by her sister-in-law in 1785.[2] Suzanne was also a gifted pianist, singer, and amateur actress. The same year that Etienne got married he was appointed to two important and lucrative positions through the influence of the Count of Vaudreuil, a favorite of Marie-Antoinette and Vigée Le Brun's most important patron during the 1780s, and Finance Minister Charles-Alexandre de Calonne (plate 4). He was named secretary to the king's sister-in-law, the Countess of Provence, as well as controller-general of the Caisse des Amortissements.[3]

Etienne Vigée was an enormously charming man, a moderately gifted author but an opportunist of the first magnitude who knew how to survive, indeed thrive, through the tumultuous decades of revolutionary and postrevolutionary France. His career and activities after 1789 attest that, in spite of his successes under the Old Regime, he did not hesitate to side with the revolutionaries, and this in spite of his sister's notorious monarchical connections and emigration. He devoted some of his most eloquent verse to celebrating the overthrow of Louis XVI, such as his 1793 *Ode à La Liberté*. He praised Napoleon in equally enthusiastic verse, and after Waterloo acclaimed Louis XVIII, who rewarded him by making him his official reader and bestowing upon him the *Légion d'Honneur*. That he had by this time condemned the Revolution should hardly surprise us. In 1803 he was called upon to succeed the famous critic and lecturer Jean-François La Harpe, another intellectual who had turned against the Revolution, in the teaching of the famous *Lycée*, a history of literature both ancient and modern, a daunting task with which he acquitted himself honorably while not quite succeeding in living up to the brilliance of his predecessor.

Elisabeth's portrait of her brother and her other early portraits set a pattern she would later follow as an artist. Above all else, she sought to achieve an effect of naturalness and spontaneity by seizing her subject in an unguarded, yet highly revealing moment of self-absorption.[4] No obvious ideological message is conveyed in this type of portraiture. For Elisabeth the intimate and inner truth of individuality is what mattered, but without conveying any sense of drama or tragedy. There is no inkling of loneliness or alienation. Her subjects are indeed caught in moments of contemplation, but their expressions convey the kind of easy sociability and amiability dear to the eighteenth-century ideal of human communication. She does not seek to capture potent moments of high emotional stress or drama. On the contrary, her subjects are appealing in that they are shown in a kind of pleasant reverie, a state of calm, introspective, silent reflexiveness. Furthermore, her general predilection for youthful subjects, especially lovely and seductively erotic young women portrayed in all the trappings of a privileged social position, reflects her concept of idealized portraiture.

Despite her warm relationship with Joseph Vernet, Hubert Robert, and especially Jean-Baptiste Greuze—whose dramatic compositions combined sentimentality and pathos, extolled family values, and epitomized moralistic painting so enthusiastically endorsed by Diderot in his *Salons*—Vigée Le Brun remained from the outset impervious to the Enlightenment belief that art should be public oriented. This personal preference would eventually coincide with her conservative politics. Indeed, in *Souvenirs* she wants to make clear that, even though her father had been on close enough terms with the circle of the Encyclopedists to dine with them, he was alarmed by their radical ideas: "How often have I recalled, especially after 1789, the following as a kind of prophecy. One day, my father upon returning from a dinner which had also been attended by Diderot, Helvétius, and D'Alembert, appeared so depressed that my mother asked him what was troubling him. 'Everything I just heard, dearest,' he answered, 'makes me believe that soon the world will be topsy-turvy'" (I, 30).

While living with her mother and detested stepfather, Elisabeth was easily able to expand her circle of friends and acquaintances. Her exceptional talent as a portraitist, coupled with her good looks, soon attracted an increasing number of visitors and potential clients. Before long she would move into the brilliant and brittle aristocratic world of privilege and pleasure. Her reputation kept growing, and increasingly important commissions came her way.

CHAPTER THREE

~ *Marriage* ~

AS A SINGULARLY GIFTED and attractive young painter, Elisabeth Vigée came on the artistic and social scene at a particularly propitious time for her type of pleasing and idealized portraiture. The fashionable French circles, always eager for new faces and new talent, began to seek her out and to invite her to dinners and other functions. Her beauty and natural graciousness easily endeared her to the nobility, and her stepfather's move to the fashionable vicinity of Palais-Royal facilitated socially useful encounters. Ladies of the court, among others the Duchess of Chartres, daughter-in-law of the Duke of Orléans, who frequently took walks in Palais-Royal, heard about her, and out of curiosity paid her visits in order to observe her at work. This would inevitably be followed by commissions to paint portraits.

Elisabeth also received the visit of the formidable Marie-Thérèse Geoffrin, then in her early seventies and hostess of a famed salon on the rue Saint-Honoré frequented by the leading men of letters and artists of the day.[1] Herself of bourgeois origin, she reigned supreme as a *salonnière*. Her gatherings brought together such literary figures as Montesquieu, Marivaux, Diderot, and D'Alembert, as well as such noted painters as Vernet, Vien, Boucher, and La Tour. As a hostess whose fame had spread beyond the French borders, she also received numerous foreign visitors, notably Horace Walpole, Prince Poniatowski, soon to become king of Poland, and the abbé Galiani, the Italian economist who made a name for himself with his *Dialogues on the Commerce of Wheat* (1770).

Even though Elisabeth's good looks attracted many admiring glances and numerous compliments, she was so totally absorbed by her art that she looked upon these flattering marks of attention as unwelcome distractions. All her life she would remain consistent in this respect, for painting would always be her overriding, all-consuming passion. In *Souvenirs* she asserts that the principles of religion and morality instilled in her by her mother protected her from an early age against would-be seducers (I, 38). She also felt that it was her good luck not to have been exposed to the reading of novels, an experience widely considered at the time as particularly threatening to the virtue of young girls, since it appealed so powerfully to their imagination and sensibilities: "The first novel I read was *Clarissa Harlowe*, which fascinated me, but I read it only after my marriage" (I, 39).

Novels were both officially condemned and immensely popular in the eighteenth century,[2] and Elisabeth Vigée's opinions in matters of politics and aesthetics were consistently and prudently conservative. And that she was willing to make an exception for Samuel Richardson's edifying and widely admired novel depicting the tragic story of a virtuous young woman who falls victim to Lovelace, her scheming and unscrupulous seducer, is entirely in keeping with her own predilection for pathos mingled with morality.

On Sundays and holidays Elisabeth and her mother and stepfather attended church and took walks in the garden of Palais-Royal, where elegant members of high society would congregate. The opera house was nearby, and in the summer spectators would sometimes leave before the end of the show in order to promenade in the garden. There would be music in the moonlight, and amateur singers performed for the public. Palais-Royal was also frequented by less respectable people, notably courtesans. "You have no idea," Vigée Le Brun remarked in *Souvenirs*, "what these kept women were like . . . Mademoiselle Duthé, for example, ate up millions" (I, 40). Her observation is corroborated by Diderot's lively description, in the beginning of *Rameau's Nephew*, of encountering in the late afternoon hours at Palais-Royal pretty, young courtesans with giddy demeanors, smiling faces, bright eyes, and cute, upturned noses.[3]

In her autobiography Vigée Le Brun recalls with much nostalgia the numerous places of recreation, in Paris itself as well as in its immediate surroundings, that she frequented as a young woman, and the various amusements available to ordinary people at that time, and she deplores the fact that the only public promenades left after the Revolution were the Tuileries and the Luxembourg Gardens (I, 45). Her obvious intent, of course, is to suggest that there was an enjoyment of life, the famous "douceur de vivre" evoked by Talleyrand, that had all but vanished with the Revolution.

Elisabeth's stepfather rented a cottage at Chaillot, where the family would spend the weekends. There she discovered the dubious pleasure of suburban life. A tiny, treeless garden provided no shelter from the sun, and she was constantly terrified by the noise emanating from neighbors awkwardly practicing their shooting skills: "I could not understand that one would call the countryside a place that is so dull and anti-picturesque and where I was so bored that I yawn just remembering it" (I, 46).

What a contrast when, thanks to the connections she was making as a rising young artist, she was invited to Marly-le-Roi, a château and gardens conceived and executed by the celebrated architect Jules Mansart for Louis XIV. Here, for the first time, Elisabeth had the revelation of beauty and grandeur in architecture and garden design. The château itself, its twelve pavilions, and the gardens with their waterfalls, everything she saw bespoke the power and glory of the age of Louis XIV and monarchy at its pinnacle. She wrote of her first undated encounter with Marie-Antoinette and her entourage of ladies-in-waiting taking a walk in this enchanting setting: "They were all in white dresses, and so young and pretty that they seemed like an apparition" (I, 47). (Later, upon returning to France in 1802 after the Revolution, Vigée Le Brun found that Marly had been totally destroyed: "The palace, the trees, the cascades, everything had disappeared" [I, 47].)

By the early 1770s, Elisabeth was intent on securing her growing reputation as a portrait painter, no easy endeavor for a woman artist. The time for fresh new talent seemed right. The art world offered a rich but complex tapestry of contradictory trends. The rococo style, with its voluptuously seductive appeal as exemplified in the playfully erotic pastorals of Boucher and Fragonard, was beginning to lose its hold on the public as well as on connoisseurs and art critics. Greuze and his edifying compositions on middle-class and rural themes, on the other hand, strongly appealed to a newfound sense of morality largely aroused by Rousseau's writings.[4] At the same time, neoclassicism was on the rise, greatly energized by Johann Joachim Winckelmann's archaeological and art history work, which projected an idealized and virile image of antiquity.[5] The neoclassical style largely represented the pictorial expression of a basic belief in the immutability and universality of beauty embodied in models selected from known masterpieces of Greco-Roman antiquity, especially statuary. This heroic, grandiose concept of art would of course find its ultimate realization in the compositions of Jacques-Louis David. The rococo style, on the other hand, was intent on capturing more subjective emotions and feelings in terms of coloristic and painterly values. Vigée Le Brun never attempted to theorize her ideas about painting, but to the extent that she greatly admired Peter Paul Rubens and his virtuosity as a colorist, and placed him on a par with such venerated masters of the Italian Renaissance as Raphael, she probably had a greater affinity with the rococo than with the more formal and austere neoclassicism. Yet her portraiture encompasses a remarkably successful melding of the major features of eighteenth-century art.

As a woman Elisabeth was not only deprived of formal academic training, she would also face formidable obstacles in attempting to gain recognition as a serious artist. She could hardly hope to be elected to the prestigious but highly conservative Académie Royale de Peinture et de Sculpture, so she therefore applied for membership in the Académie de Saint Luc, the respectable relative of the Académie. Her father had been a member, and this may well have prompted her to apply herself. In August and September of 1774 she exhibited a number of compositions at the Salon de Saint Luc, and her official reception took place in October of that year. This was at least partial recognition of her exceptional abilities.

Elisabeth was ambitious and hardly at a loss to find new stratagems to gain official recognition of her talent. To gain the goodwill of no less an august body than the Académie she conceived the idea of submitting portraits of two important figures in French history and literature, based on engravings and offered in homage to the Académie. The two selected figures were the cleric-statesman Cardinal de Fleury and the moralist La Bruyère, both of whom had been omitted from the official portraits of the Académie. D'Alembert, the celebrated mathematician, Perpetual Secretary of the French Academy, and co-editor with Diderot of the *Encyclopédie*, wrote her a florid letter of thanks in the name of the Académie, and even went so far as to pay her a personal visit. He struck her as a man of small stature and cold demeanor, but one with exquisite manners: "He stayed a long time in my atelier and told me a thousand flattering things" (I, 52). Vigée Le Brun could not resist mentioning in *Souvenirs* this connection with one of the leading Enlightenment *philosophes*, and even quoting in full his letter to her (I, 51–52). It is noteworthy that, as portraitist of Marie-Antoinette, émigrée, and staunch monarchist she could never quite bring herself to renege on her early personal and artistic ties with some of the leaders of the Enlightenment movement.

While Elisabeth's reputation was growing, the money she was earning was being unscrupulously pocketed by her avaricious stepfather, who, upon retirement from his jewelry business, gave up his apartment in the rue Saint-Honoré for a home in the Hôtel de Lubert on the somewhat less fashionable rue de Cléry. Some of the residents were nevertheless fairly notable or seemingly well-off; one of them was Jean-Baptiste-Pierre Le Brun, who was the son of an antiques dealer and a great-nephew of Charles Le Brun, the seventeenth-century classical painter, decorator, and protégé of Jean-Baptiste Colbert. Charles was known primarily for his epic mural paintings at Versailles and the Louvre (Galerie d'Apollon). As director of the Académie Royale de Peinture et de Sculpture, he dominated artistic production and theory and staunchly defended the grand manner until his death in 1690, which was followed by the rise of the rococo style. Jean-Baptiste-Pierre himself was a painter in his own right, albeit one whose fairly limited abilities could hardly measure up with those of his famous great-uncle. Above all he was an art dealer in old masters.[6]

Le Brun was Elisabeth's senior by seven years, and he gradually won her over by his flattering attentiveness and by the readiness with which he encouraged her to visit and copy from his considerable collection of fine old paintings. When he proposed marriage, however, she at first hesitated, for at twenty years of age she was already earning a handsome income and felt secure in her own future. Moreover, as she recalled in *Souvenirs*, she "had no special desire to get married" (I, 53). In this defiant attitude she obviously differed markedly from her contemporaries.

Unlike the vast majority of young women, who languished at home in idleness and boredom while awaiting a suitable match, Elisabeth had acquired a measure of personal independence thanks to her exceptional talent as an artist. She found in her art as well as in the social connections it afforded a great source of personal pleasure and gratification. She fully enjoyed the perks and privileges that came with her growing reputation as something of a phenomenon. Furthermore, she was proud of the name she had already made for herself and did not relish the thought of exchanging it for a new one.

Marriage, therefore, was far from her mind. Her mother, however, believing Le Brun to be rich, repeatedly urged her to accept the proposal. In order to please her mother, and especially to escape from her hated stepfather, she reluctantly opted for marriage. Yet she was so unwilling to give up her freedom that she hesitated until the last moment, and even while on her way to church for the marriage ceremony she kept asking herself: "Shall I say yes? Shall I say no? Alas, I said yes, and I exchanged my troubles for other troubles" (I, 54). Her quandary is all the more understandable in light of prerevolutionary laws governing marriage, which made women totally dependent on their husbands, financially as well as in every other way.[7]

That Le Brun was an influential art dealer may have been the decisive factor in Elisabeth's decision to marry him. She probably surmised that his expertise and connections would facilitate and further her own career as a woman artist. The marriage took place on January 11, 1776, in the Paris Church of Saint Eustache. For a while the Le Bruns enjoyed a relatively stable relationship. They were far from well-off in real financial assets, however, for Le Brun had been adept at letting people, notably Elisabeth's mother, believe that he was far more successful than he actually was—for instance he misled her to believe that he owned the house on the rue de Cléry, whereas he was merely one of its tenants. But in his somewhat precarious situation Le Brun shrewdly calculated that marrying a remarkably successful young painter would bring him considerable financial and social advantages because, according to the laws governing marriage in Old Regime France, the husband represented the supreme authority in the family and exercised absolute control over its finances from the day of the marriage. Indeed, in her autobiography Vigée Le Brun claims that when she emigrated from France in 1789 she left with barely twenty francs of the more than a million she had earned as a portraitist, for her husband had squandered it all (I, 54).

In *Souvenirs* Vigée Le Brun presents herself as the victim, not only of her husband's philandering ways and passion for gambling, but also of the fact that her considerable earnings automatically became his. He was indeed a spendthrift, womanizer, and inveterate gambler. In order to increase his wife's income he even conceived the notion that she should have students. She reluctantly consented to this arrangement, and before she knew it a number of eager young women appeared at her atelier, ready for her to demonstrate how to draw eyes and noses, a task for which she felt no special calling and which distracted her from her own work (I, 55). She was singularly intent on furthering her own career, and the idea of forming a school of disciples did not particularly appeal to her.

Yet in *Souvenirs* one pupil is singled out for special mention, Marie-Guilhemine de Laville Leroulx (1768–1826), who under her married name of Benoist became a painter of history and portraitist of some renown during the tumultuous revolutionary and Napoleonic eras. Probably Benoist's best-known work is a striking portrait of a handsome young black woman, shown seated and facing the onlooker and wearing a white turban and white dress, which starkly contrast with her smooth, ebony complexion. The portrait, titled *Portrait of a Negress*, created something of a sensation at the Salon of 1800 and is now in the Louvre (fig. 1).

Yet the case of Benoist illustrates the extraordinary difficulties women artists faced in pursuing an artistic career. She successfully exhibited history paintings in the Salon of 1791, received numerous commissions from Napoleon, was the recipient of the gold medal in 1804,

FIG. 1. *Marie-Guilhemine Benoist*, Portrait of a Negress, *1800. Musée National du Louvre, Paris. (Réunion des Musées Nationaux/Art Resource, NY)*

and was granted an annual stipend—along with other noted artists such as Antoine Gros and Pierre Prud'hon—by the Napoleonic regime. Yet after the fall of Napoleon her husband, Pierre-Vincent Benoist, was appointed to the exalted post of Conseiller d'Etat in the Restoration regime with the condition that his wife give up her career as a painter.[8]

Le Brun was one of the major dealers in a growing and increasingly sophisticated Parisian art market. He generally favored the old Italian masters as the best financial investments for his clients. At the same time he was a keen connoisseur of Dutch and Flemish painters, and this expertise doubtless contributed to his wife's knowledge and appreciation of these artists of the so-called Northern School, especially Rubens, one of her principal inspirations as a colorist.

In a self-portrait dated 1795 Le Brun represents himself in his dual roles as artist and art connoisseur (fig. 2). In his left hand he holds a palette, while his right hand rests on a volume of engravings. In the eighteenth century men who had made great fortunes were eager to invest in bankable works of art. These early capitalists were Le Brun's best clients. But his problem was that he always lived above his means and spent money more quickly than it came in. Thanks to his wife's increasing earnings, however, he was able to enlarge his collection and keep his business going. The house that the Le Bruns occupied on the rue de Cléry offered an impressive display of luxury and art that had little connection with the financial realities of the couple. If Elisabeth's marriage turned out to be a personal failure, it nevertheless helped to further her career as an artist, for it opened doors that otherwise would most probably have remained shut had she chosen to remain a single woman artist.

The union produced one offspring, a girl named Julie (her full name was Jeanne-Julie-Louise), born on February 12, 1780. The expectant mother was so involved in her work that she made no preparations for the birth and stubbornly refused to leave her easel until labor pains

FIG. 2. *Jean-Baptiste-Pierre Le Brun (husband of the artist)*, Self-Portrait, *1795. Private collection. (Courtesy of the Wildenstein Institute, Paris)*

actually overwhelmed her. An *accoucheur* was promptly sent for, and as Vigée Le Brun recalls her delivery: "I shall not try to describe the joy I experienced upon hearing the first cries of my child. All mothers know this exhilaration" (I, 59).

Julie was a pretty, vivacious little girl, and her mother took delight in painting and sketching her repeatedly, either alone or in the warmly protective embrace of her mother's arms (see plate 12). Vigée Le Brun tried her best to be a good mother, but the enormous demands made upon her as an artist greatly encroached upon the time and energy she could devote to her daughter, a factor that probably contributed to their later difficult relationship. On the other hand, the experience of motherhood considerably enriched her inspiration as a painter. Indeed, maternal love became a central theme in her portraits of young women, especially of herself with Julie and of Marie-Antoinette with her children. Some of her most famous paintings represent her lovingly enfolding Julie in a warm, protective embrace.

Rousseau had ushered in the age of sensibility with his immensely popular novel *Julie, ou la nouvelle Héloïse* (1761), and, like so many other women of her generation, Vigée Le Brun strongly responded to his touching and eloquent advocacy of family values. That she never manifested the slightest interest in Rousseau's political writings, such as *The Social Contract*, is, of course, hardly surprising.[9]

Vigée Le Brun was intuitively attuned to the complex cultural currents of her time. The last decades of the Old Regime witnessed a growing disenchantment and weariness with libertine sophistication and cynicism, religious skepticism and incredulity, and a nostalgic yearning for a return to a simpler, more innocent way of life. If Vigée Le Brun repeatedly treated the maternity topic in paintings of herself and other young women, including Marie-Antoinette, it probably is because she realized that she could convey a powerful as well as enticingly seductive message that would resonate with the public, since it would irresistibly evoke a familiar iconographic tradition of the Madonna and Child.

Vigée Le Brun's success was such that would-be portrait sitters of the highest ranks lined up to get their turn. Her clientele included the high and mighty, as well as royal mistresses, notably Madame du Barry, who was in her mid-forties when she was first introduced to her portraitist. In her autobiography Vigée Le Brun aptly and succinctly summarizes du Barry's career in the following terms: "A woman who came from the lowest ranks of society and who went from a royal palace to the scaffold" (I, 123).

Madame du Barry was an ex-mistress of the deceased Louis XV when she first sat for Vigée Le Brun in 1781, wearing an informal dressing robe of white muslin and a straw hat in the English style embellished with plumes (France, private collection). Vigée Le Brun was understandably fascinated by the former mistress of Louis XV: "She was fairly tall, on the plump side and full-bosomed; her face was still charming; her features were regular and graceful; her hair was ash-colored and curly like those of a child" (I, 124).

Du Barry was a gracious hostess in Louveciennes, a small town near Versailles where she resided in a private estate built for her by Louis XV and where, according to Vigée Le Brun, she led a simple existence and tried her best to help the destitute: "We often went together to visit some unfortunates, and I still remember her anger when she once saw a poor woman who had recently given birth and who lacked everything" (I, 125). At the same time, however, du Barry was not only reluctant to reveal any detail about her relationship with Louis XV, she also betrayed infantile mannerisms and a certain intellectual vacuousness: "Her gaze was that of a coquette, her slanted eyes were never completely open, and her pronunciation had something childish which did not suit her age" (I, 124).

Vigée Le Brun painted three portraits of Madame du Barry. In addition to the 1781 portrait, in 1782 she executed a full-length portrait of her facing the viewer, dressed in white satin, holding a wreath in her right hand, and lightly leaning her left arm on a pedestal (plate 5). But when, in 1789, Vigée Le Brun undertook a third portrait it was abruptly interrupted by the dramatic events of the French Revolution. Having to flee from France precipitously, she left her painting unfinished. By a stroke of good luck, however, it was preserved in her absence, and she completed it around 1820 (private collection).

Unlike his wife, Le Brun chose to remain in revolutionary France, probably less for ideological reasons than in order to protect his business, art collection, and house on the rue de Cléry (which he had bought thanks to Elisabeth's handsome income). Besides, he surmised that with the collapse of the Old Regime and the emigration of so many aristocrats there would be numerous opportunities to acquire works of art at bargain prices. But he failed to make the expected profits, for in this time of crisis and uncertainty there were very few buyers. Le Brun found himself so financially strapped that on April 11, 1791, he had to sell his collection of paintings, drawings, art objects, and fine furniture.

Furthermore, the fact that Le Brun was the husband of a notorious émigré would make his life increasingly difficult. Vigée Le Brun's emigration would cause her to lose all her rights as a citizen. In spite of unreliability in sexual and financial matters, Le Brun turned out to be remarkably and even courageously loyal to his wife. In August 1792 he formally but unsuccessfully requested the Legislative Assembly to remove her name from the list of émigrés, and he steadfastly defended her in the face of the mounting Terror in the form of numerous petitions defending her moral character against the calumnies spread by her enemies.[10]

Le Brun benefited from personal connections that protected him from persecution, notably that of Jacques-Louis David, virtual art dictator during the French Revolution. His expertise would be further acknowledged by the revolutionaries when they would appoint him member of a committee whose task it was to select art works worthy of preservation. In this capacity Le Brun managed to save a number of monuments and art works from destruction.

In 1794, at the height of the Terror, Le Brun finally found himself forced to sue his wife for divorce on the grounds of desertion. One of the last acts of the Legislative Assembly was the law of September 20, 1792, establishing divorce. On June 3, 1794, a decree of divorce was issued for the Le Bruns. Yet when, in 1802, Vigée Le Brun finally returned to France after pursuing a phenomenally successful career as a portraitist all over Europe, for the sake of convenience she would resume living with her ex-husband in their house on the rue de Cléry.

CHAPTER FOUR

Marie-Antoinette's Portraitist

As VIGÉE LE BRUN's reputation grew, Versailles became increasingly aware of her existence (plate 6). She painted her first portrait of Marie-Antoinette in 1778, *Marie-Antoinette "en robe à paniers"* (plate 7). This is a full-length, formal representation of the queen in court regalia, wearing a splendidly decorated white satin hoopskirt. While the portrait brilliantly demonstrates Vigée Le Brun's virtuosity as a court painter, it reveals little of its subject. But it was eminently in keeping with a tradition of formal portraiture of the spouse of a monarch. The portrait was executed for the queen's brother, Emperor Joseph II, and Marie-Antoinette was so pleased with it that she ordered two copies: one for Catherine II, Empress of all Russias, and the other for her own apartments at Versailles.

During the first sitting for this portrait Vigée Le Brun was enormously intimidated, but the queen spoke to her with reassuring kindness and graciousness (I, 65). This marked the beginning of a growing personal relationship between the artist and the monarch, who was then in the full bloom of her youth and beauty. In her memoir Vigée Le Brun speaks glowingly and nostalgically of the sensitivity and consideration with which Marie-Antoinette invariably treated her, and offers several examples of the friendship and intimacy that were soon established between these two women with such disparate backgrounds. Having learned that Vigée Le Brun had a pleasing singing voice, Marie-Antoinette, who loved music although she herself was not endowed with a particularly good voice, would almost always conclude their sessions by joining with her in a duo. One of their favorite composers was André Grétry, a master of eighteenth-century opéra comique whose works combined the melodic grace of Italian opera with the dramatic interest of the French.

On one occasion Vigée Le Brun unexpectedly missed an appointment for a sitting; pregnant at the time, she felt too ill to make the trip to Versailles. The following day she hurried to Versailles to offer her apologies. The queen did not expect her and was finishing her toilette before taking a ride in her carriage. Upon learning that her portraitist had come to make an appointment for another day, she readily received her and, after gently chiding her, gave orders to cancel her promenade for a sitting: "I remember that in my eagerness to respond to this kindness, I seized my paintbox with such a rush that it spilled; my brushes fell on the floor; I kneeled down . . . 'Leave everything,' said the Queen, 'You are too advanced in your pregnancy to bend down.' And she then proceeded to pick up everything herself" (I, 68).

Gradually Vigée Le Brun became the queen's favorite artist and *portraitiste en titre* (official portraitist), and in this capacity she was able to exercise increasing freedom in her style of portraiture. For instance, the 1783 portrait known as *Marie-Antoinette "en gaule"* (plate 8) is a close-up and intimate three-quarter-length portrait of an attractive young woman wearing an informal white muslin dress and a broad-rimmed, plumed hat. She is holding a rose in her left hand. When exhibited in the Salon the portrait provoked unflattering comments, and wagging tongues maliciously spread the rumor that the queen had had herself painted in her nightgown.

Rose Bertin, the queen's dressmaker, had urged her to give up the stiff formal court dress in favor of loose-fitting, simple gowns of white cotton or muslin, and the queen was eager to give up the enormous hooped skirts and the elaborately structured coiffures. She banished them from the court, except for special occasions. Vigée Le Brun, for her part, eagerly welcomed this opportunity to represent the queen not merely as an impersonal symbol of royalty, but as a woman in all her appealing and vulnerable femininity. This unexpectedly unconventional representation of the queen of France was not well received, and it provoked something of a scandal and even contributed to her growing unpopularity and to the spreading of malicious gossip about her moral character.

In *Souvenirs* Vigée Le Brun presents a striking portrait of the queen in her prime. She describes her as tall and admirably well proportioned, with a natural majesty in her demeanor: "Her features were not regular; she had inherited from her family a narrow oval face peculiar to the Austrian nation. She had rather small eyes bluish in tinge; her gaze was both witty and gentle, her nose fine and pretty, and her mouth not too large, although her lips were a bit too full. But what is most remarkable in her face is her complexion. I have never seen anything so brilliant, and brilliant is the right word, for her skin was so transparent that it did not catch any shadow. As a result, I could never render its effect satisfactorily. Colors failed me to paint this freshness, these unbelievably subtle tones that I have never found in any other woman" (I, 64–5).

Vigée Le Brun was indeed proud of the close relationship she was able to establish with the queen, and her intention was doubtless to demonstrate the fact that an absolute monarch could properly honor and further the career of an artist, a tradition going back to the Italian Renaissance. What was unusual in this case was that the relationship was between two women. In spite of their very disparate social situations, they shared mutual respect and sympathy and probably also a common sense of frustration as unhappily married women and as targets of increasingly vicious calumnies, one as a foreigner—*l'Autrichienne* (the Austrian woman)—and the other as a woman artist intent on making a name for herself in a world overwhelmingly dominated by men. Indeed their friendly relationship fed the prevalent malicious rumors about the queen's purported promiscuity, questionable sexuality, and lesbian tendencies.[1] That one of her favorite and intimate companions was the lovely Duchess Yolande de Polignac (plate 10) greatly contributed to these rumors.

As for the painter's attachment to her royal subject, it remained fiercely loyal, especially after Marie-Antoinette's cruel death. In her memoir Vigée Le Brun is obviously intent on rehabilitating the queen's reputation by recounting several anecdotes intended to underscore her kindly, generous nature and the goodness of her heart, especially in her dealings with ordinary people, as when she made sure that her daughter, Marie-Thérèse Charlotte de France, then aged six, properly honored a little peasant girl whom she had invited to dinner by serving her first (I, 68).[2]

Vigée Le Brun was commissioned to paint a large number of portraits of Marie-Antoinette, both formal and informal. In each case she was consistently able to convey a sympathetic, vivid representation of a queen as a sensitive, thoughtful young woman. Even in more sumptuous, regal portraits, such as the *Marie-Antoinette "en robe de velours bleu"* (1788, Collection Bronson Trevor), she is at once a figure of quiet self-confident authority and of dignified femininity. She is seated holding a book in her left hand, indicating her serious interests, and she lightly rests her right hand on a table bearing a vase of flowers. Her elaborate headdress is topped with ornamental plumes. The composition has a baroque, quasi-theatrical element to it, with its background of column and drapery. Yet the personality of the queen strongly dominates the composition.

In the famous *Marie-Antoinette and Her Children* (plate 11), the queen is represented as a contented mother surrounded by her brood. The composition was probably meant partially to rehabilitate Marie-Antoinette's tarnished image and help ward off the growing public animosity directed at her. More importantly, it constitutes a translation in pictorial terms of a moral and bourgeois ideal of motherhood and family values propounded by such Enlightenment philosophes as Diderot and Rousseau. Greuze, one of Vigée Le Brun's mentors and supporters, had for his part achieved great success with compositions depicting endearing or dramatic family scenes.

In *Marie-Antoinette and Her Children,* Vigée Le Brun is intent on conveying a political message by integrating this moralistic, bourgeois ideal and family values into the context of absolute monarchy. The queen is shown seated, gently cradling in her arms her youngest child, Louis-Charles, Duc de Normandie, who, after his father was guillotined, became known as Louis XVII and died under mysterious circumstances. Standing next to their mother are, to her right, Marie-Thérèse, also known as Madame Royale, and, to the queen's left, Louis-Joseph, the Dauphin, pointing at an empty cradle, a reference to Princess Sophie, who had died shortly after her birth in 1786.

Between May and June of 1781 Vigée Le Brun accompanied her husband on a business tour of Flanders and Holland. In addition to being introduced to members of the high society of Brussels and viewing some superb art collections, notably that of Charles-Joseph de Ligne, French aristocrat, soldier, and man of letters who graciously hosted the couple in his superb estate of Beloeil, she was especially impressed by the magnificent Van Dycks and, above all, by the Rubens masterpieces in Flemish churches, galleries, and private collections.[3]

In Antwerp she came upon Rubens's masterful portrait of his sister-in-law, Susanna Lunden, the older sister of Hélène Fourment, who became the painter's second wife in 1630 (London, National Gallery).[4] The portrait produced such an impact on her that, while still in Brussels, she painted a self-portrait largely inspired by this composition (I, 34). It is known as *Self-Portrait with a Straw Hat* (plate 9).

Vigée Le Brun's self-portrait is a worthy homage to Rubens's brilliant virtuosity as a colorist, and it strove to achieve similar effects of light and color. As in the Rubens painting, the setting is out of doors, enabling the artist to depict natural lighting, so that even the shadow of the subject's plumed hat barely affects the brightness of her skin. And in her portrait there is a real *chapeau de paille* (straw hat), unlike Rubens's subject, whose hat was actually of beaver felt. To the dashing ostrich feather the artist added a wreath of freshly picked rustic flowers. And where Susanna Lunden peers at us in a coyly indirect fashion, Vigée Le Brun directly meets our gaze with self-assurance, and her lips are partly open in an inviting smile. Unlike Rubens's subject, whose breasts are pushed high and close together by a tight corset, Vigée Le Brun displays a low and free décolletage. Finally, while Lunden keeps her arms and hands demurely and idly crossed above her waist, Vigée Le Brun extends her right hand in an open, welcoming gesture, while her left hand firmly grips a palette and brushes, a proud and self-confident proclamation of herself as both subject and artist.

In her memoir Vigée Le Brun notes with undisguised satisfaction that her *Self-Portrait in a Straw Hat* was largely instrumental in her election to the Académie Royale de Peinture et de Sculpture in 1783. She emphasizes the fact that the initiative did not come from her but rather from one of her mentors, the painter Joseph Vernet (I, 76). This was indeed a bold move, since women had never achieved this distinction. But by then she strongly felt that she had earned this right, and her goal was to achieve membership, not merely as portraitist, traditionally viewed as a minor and inferior genre in the classical academic hierarchy, but as a full-fledged history painter.

But if Vigée Le Brun had supporters among painters, she also had powerful enemies. One of the most vocal adversaries and fiercest opponents to her election was Jean-Baptiste Pierre, now largely and justifiably forgotten but then an influential and successful history painter who cumulated various official functions, notably as Professor at the Royal Academy and First Painter of the king. To be sure, the authoritarian Pierre had his own critics, notably Diderot, who looked upon him as the quintessential court painter who made the most of his limited talent and lack of originality by skillfully exploiting an ability to treat and at times plagiarize historical and religious themes. In fact, Diderot took a mischievous pleasure in repeatedly ridiculing Pierre in his *Salons*.[5]

For an exceptionally talented painter like Vigée Le Brun, election to the Académie Royale de Peinture et de Sculpture was a primary goal, for among other privileges it would give her the right to exhibit her paintings in the biennial Salon at the Louvre. Yet, the Académie was most reluctant to accept women painters as members, and to relent would be an exception to the rule. Furthermore, by tradition and law Academicians did not engage in art-related commerce, and she could therefore be barred from the Académie as the wife of an art dealer.

As a reception piece Vigée Le Brun submitted *Peace Bringing Back Abundance*, painted in 1780, in order to demonstrate that she was fully capable of executing this kind of allegorical painting with brilliance and brio, and therefore that she had earned the credentials as a full-fledged history painter and not merely as a portraitist (fig. 3). In spite of its traditional symbolism, the dynamic composition has an all-embracing sweep, and the two attractive female figures, representing peace and abundance, respectively, are linked in a common vigorous upward motion, with the figure of peace gently guiding and protecting peace.

On May 31, 1783, Vigée Le Brun was accorded full membership, thanks largely to the direct intervention of Marie-Antoinette.[6] In *Souvenirs* she minimizes the queen's role, although she diplomatically acknowledges that both "the King and Queen had been good enough to

FIG. 3. *Elisabeth Vigée Le Brun*, Peace Bringing Back Abundance, *1780. Musée National du Louvre, Paris. (Réunion des Musées Nationaux/Art Resource, NY)*

wish to see me enter the Academy" (I, 77). Her uncanny combination of exceptional talent and astuteness had finally paid off. She had further-more adroitly manipulated royal patronage by paying strict adherence to moral propriety, a timely strategy in view of Marie-Antoinette's already badly tainted reputation.

All the elaborate precautions Vigée Le Brun took to protect her own public image, however, did not prevent scandalmongers from exploiting her connection with the great and powerful. One of the malicious rumors was that she had a sexual relationship with Count Charles-Alexandre de Calonne, Louis XVI's finance minister from 1783 until 1787, whose portrait she painted in 1784 (see plate 4) and whose collection of French and Dutch masters had been largely acquired through the services of the artist's husband-dealer.[7] Vigée Le Brun consistently and vigorously denied this rumor, insisting that she as an artist and Calonne as a politician had little in common and no reason for mutual attraction, and furthermore, that she hardly knew him personally. Calonne was a very busy man, and sittings for his portrait had to be shortened (I, 94). Whether her protestations are entirely truthful is impossible to ascertain. What can reasonably be assumed is that her overriding passion throughout her life was her calling as an artist, and this was most probably the case when, as an ambitious young painter, she was struggling mightily and pouring all her energies into asserting herself as a painter of the first rank.

As for Calonne, he was dismissed in 1787, for he had not only failed in his controversial attempt to deal with the huge public debt and deteriorating financial situation by adopting a spending policy that was followed by a brief period of prosperity before a ruinous collapse, he was also accused of misusing public money on a grand scale. Not too surprisingly, after 1789 he was looked upon as one of the principal evildoers of the Old Regime.[8]

Be that as it may, Vigée Le Brun's portrait of Calonne is a masterful example of the official court portrait, or *portrait d'apparat*, which she nevertheless succeeded in humanizing (see plate 4). The handsome, youthful minister, bewigged and elegantly attired in black satin, poses seated at his working desk, holding a document in his left hand and facing us with a quiet look of authority and self-confidence.

Yet another malicious rumor that circulated was specifically intended to damage her reputation as an artist: she was accused of not being the actual author of the paintings attributed to her. Rather, she allegedly received considerable help in the execution of her portraits from more experienced male painters, notably from a respectable history painter, François-Guillaume Ménageot. Unfortunately for Vigée

Le Brun, Ménageot happened to reside in the same house on the rue de Cléry where she and her husband also lived.[9]

By an interesting coincidence, Vigée Le Brun's admission to the Académie occurred simultaneously with that of another woman artist, Adélaïde Labille-Guiard (1749–1803).[10] Labille-Guiard had also achieved renown as a portraitist of exceptional talent. Like Vigée Le Brun, she, too, was the target of libelous attacks and vicious accusations, notably that she passed off as her own paintings those by François-André Vincent, a history painter who happened to be her friend and mentor and, eventually, her second husband.[11]

Labille-Guiard had less facility and panache than Vigée Le Brun. Her portraits are serious, sober, straightforward representations of their subjects. Her color scheme is also more muted and less brilliant than that of Vigée Le Brun. She did not idealize or flatter her subjects, who are represented in a straightforward, uncompromising way. A good case in point is her 1782 *Self-Portrait*, which, perhaps not coincidentally, was hung next to Vigée Le Brun's glamorous *Self-Portrait in a Straw Hat* at the Salon de la Correspondance.

The two self-portraits are an interesting study in subtly contrasting styles. Both self-portraits represent attractive young women artists holding a palette and brushes in their left hand and facing the onlooker with an air of quiet self-confidence. But whereas Labille-Guiard strikes a generally demure, self-contained, and modest post, Vigée Le Brun is far more assertive in the way she boldly asserts her femininity in her frontal pose and boldly exposed décolletage.

Although Labille-Guiard eventually became the official portraitist of Louis XVI's aunts, Madame Victoire and Madame Adélaïde, this could hardly compete with Vigée Le Brun's spectacular success as official portraitist of Marie-Antoinette. When both women were simultaneously elected to the Académie Royale, yet another rumor was widely circulated that, whereas Vigée Le Brun owed her election primarily to the powerful influence of Marie-Antoinette, Labille-Guiard made it strictly on her own.

The two women ultimately came to be viewed as rivals. Vigée Le Brun was doubtless the more fashionable painter, yet she was also the one embroiled in controversy because of her connection with Marie-Antoinette. Labille-Guiard never even came close to achieving Vigée Le Brun's celebrity and notoriety. Although gossips eagerly exploited the rivalry, there is no evidence of personal animosity. Still, Le Brun's remark about some artists who "would not forgive me for being the fashion and selling my pictures at better prices than theirs" (I, 90) might be an indirect reference. Their destinies also took very divergent paths during the Revolution. Whereas Vigée Le Brun opted for exile, Labille-Guiard stayed in Paris and readily espoused the revolutionary ideology.

CHAPTER FIVE

⁂ *Vigée Le Brun* Salonnière ⁂

JUST AS SOCIABILITY permeated the art of Vigée Le Brun, it was also an important factor that motivated her to become a *salonnière*. Her ideal of happiness, of easy, spontaneous, and friendly communication with kindred souls is at the root of her salon. As the wife of an ambitious art dealer she also doubtless realized that a salon would be helpful to both her own career and her husband's business.[1] Salons were presided over by women of culture and wit who also happened to have the right connections with men of power or exceptional achievement. Among the most famous and influential salons were those of Madame de Tencin, sister of a cardinal yet notorious for her scandalous lifestyle; Madame du Deffand, friend of Voltaire and Horace Walpole; Madame Geoffrin, who especially welcomed artists; and the proper, Swiss-born Madame Necker, wife of Louis XVI's director of finances and mother of Germaine de Staël. It is in the salons that the art of conversation flourished and that writers, artists, and musicians found stimulation in a relatively unfettered exchange of ideas.

Vigée Le Brun's salon is unique, however, in that it was hosted by a woman artist at the height of her creative powers. Indeed, this aspect of her life has hardly been touched upon. Between 1783, the year she was grudgingly admitted to the Académie, and 1789, her salon was highly successful, catering mainly to the fashionable and aristocratic members of French society. While she painted furiously during the daytime, sometimes combining three sessions in a single day, she would take a nap after a light meal and then seek relaxation and pleasant stimulation in the evening (I, 78). The doors of the most exclusive mansions were open to her, but dining out after a strenuous day's work was hardly what she looked for. Hence her decision to host a salon of her own.

Of course, one could hardly expect to see such representatives of the Enlightenment movement as Diderot or d'Alembert frequent the salon of a protégé of Marie-Antoinette. Rather, her guests were noble men and women who had been sufficiently impressed by her achievements and notoriety to deign grace her salon by their presence. To be sure, as Vigée Le Brun ruefully notes in *Souvenirs*, she fully realized that these grand personages probably attended her soirées less in order to see her than in order to see one another (I, 79).

In *Souvenirs* Vigée Le Brun also boasts that not only great ladies and lords, but also leading men in the world of the arts and letters vied to be invited to her salon on the rue de Cléry. While far from opulent, and certainly not on a par with the great mansions of the rich and titled of the day, the Le Brun townhouse was decorated with fine artifacts and paintings, some of which were by Rubens and Van Dyck, Vigée Le Brun's favorite masters. Her own handsome income enabled her to entertain her guests in a manner befitting their exalted social position or distinguished literary, artistic, or musical status, although in her autobiography she strenuously denies that her soirées and supper parties were extravagant affairs, contrary to rumors that were maliciously spread about them.

The graciousness of the hostess and her well-chosen entertainment in the form of poetry readings or musical recitals ensured the success of these soirées. It was when she organized concerts that she attracted the largest attendance from both the Parisian intellectual and artistic circles and from the nobility with powerful Versailles connections. Among her titled guests were such notable personalities as the Maréchal de Noailles, the Vicomte de Ségur, the Marquis de Montesquiou, the Prince de Ligne, Catherine Grand (future Princesse de Talleyrand), the Chevalier de Boufflers, and, of course, the Comte de Vaudreuil, one of her most enthusiastic patrons (figs. 4, 5). Vaudreuil's portrait, painted in 1784, shows a handsome, youthful looking man, bemedaled and in full regalia. He was especially influential at the court and close to Marie-Antoinette. He came from a West Indian family of planters that had amassed a vast sugar fortune, and his mistress, Yolande de Polignac, was the queen's favorite. It was even whispered that the two women had a lesbian relationship.

Among Le Brun's other habitués were such highly regarded poets as Jacques Delille, author of the *Jardins,* which presaged a lyrical and romantic return to nature, and Ecouchard Lebrun, surnamed Lebrun-Pindare because of his *Odes.*[2] They both excelled at reciting their verses with great rhetorical effect. Chamfort, the author of *Maximes,* witty and frequently cruel aphorisms about human frailties in the tradition of La Rochefoucauld, was another frequent guest, and he enjoyed adding zest and piquancy to the conversation with a provocative remark. Women of verve and spirit were also welcomed, especially among the aristocratic ladies Vigée Le Brun had befriended through her connection with Versailles.

In aesthetics and art criticism a strong reaction against the rococo style had set in as early as the 1750s. Proponents called for a return to noble subjects, an elevated, austere style and the *grand goût* of the preceding century (as exemplified by the classical compositions of Poussin and Le Sueur). These individuals included the antiquarian Caylus, the critic La Font de Saint-Yenne, the engraver and theorist Cochin, and

FIG. 4. *Elisabeth Vigée Le Brun*, Catherine Grand, Future Princesse de Talley-rand, *1783. The Metropolitan Museum of Art, New York. Bequest of Edward S. Harkness, 1940. (All Rights Reserved, The Metropolitan Museum of Art).*

FIG. 5. *Elisabeth Vigée Le Brun*, Portrait of Joseph-Hyacinthe-François de Vaudreuil, *1784. Virginia Museum of Fine Arts, Richmond. Gift of Mrs. A. D. Williams. (Photo: Katherine Wetzel. © Virginia Museum of Fine Arts)*

especially Diderot, who in his *Salons* launched into eloquent diatribes against Boucher and Fragonard as corrupters of true taste and cynical practitioners and exploiters of an art that reflected a heedlessly hedonistic society.[3]

By the time Vigée Le Brun came upon the artistic scene, antiquity had become a Paris fashion, and the neoclassical style was eagerly endorsed by such painters as Vien, David's teacher. Mindful of this trend, Vigée Le Brun endeavored to give her soirées a "Greek" cachet. She nostalgically describes one such evening in *Souvenirs* (I, 85–9). Women guests were enjoined to drape themselves in loose-fitting garments, and their male counterparts had to replace their wigs with more poetic wreaths of laurels, and dress in togas. As for Le Brun, since she always wore white muslin dresses, all she needed to do was add a veil and place a wreath of flowers on her head. She took special pleasure in decking out her daughter, Julie, in similar fashion. Dishes were prepared in accordance with ancient recipes, and old wines were imported from Cyprus and served in genuine Etruscan vases and cups provided by a collector-friend. Arias from Christoph Willibald Gluck were sung to the accompaniment of a lyre. The selection of Gluck was no coincidence. A German born composer, Gluck had been young Marie-Antoinette's music teacher at the Austrian court of her mother, the Empress Maria Teresa, and had come to Paris in order to follow his imperial pupil, who was of considerable help to him in overcoming the hostility of the French and their partiality for Rameau, one of their own composers, and in introducing a new style of opera fusing dramatic, emotional, and musical elements, notably in *Iphigénie en Aulide* (1774) and *Iphigénie en Taulide* (1779). The evening was topped off by Lebrun-Pindare reciting to great effect his own translations of several odes by the Greek lyric poet Anacreon. Even Chateaubriand, in his *Memoirs from Beyond the Tomb*, evokes both Vigée Le Brun's famous "Greek supper" and the part Lebrun-Pindare played in it, a laurel wreath on his head and a lyre in his hand.[4]

The evening was a sensational success, and Vigée Le Brun was urged to repeat her Greek supper. Prudently she refused, for she realized that there were those who, out of envy or because of her close association with an increasingly unpopular queen, wished her ill and were eager to spread slanderous rumors about her: "Although I was, I believe, the most harmless being that ever existed, I had enemies" (I, 90).

That her activities were scrutinized and her soirées closely monitored is attested to by the fact that her Greek supper was promptly reported to the king, who, concerned over the reputation of the queen and her entourage for extravagance, expressed some annoyance over its apparent cost (I, 88). No wonder, therefore, that Vigée Le Brun turned down suggestions by ladies of the court to repeat the performance, even at the risk of offending them.

In spite of these precautions, however, word soon spread that Vigée Le Brun's Greek supper had involved a huge expenditure of money, something she strenuously denied, insisting that the expense had been minimal and that the evening had been such a success primarily because of her imaginative improvisation (I, 88). Nonetheless, malicious rumors persisted. In Versailles the sum was reported to have been twenty-thousand francs, and it was soon even more inflated as gossip spread throughout Europe and reached such foreign capitals as Rome, Vienna, and far-off St. Petersburg, where the rumor of the event's cost ballooned to no less than eighty-thousand francs.[5] No wonder that Vigée Le Brun constantly endeavored to run a salon that would remain politically and ideologically above reproach and that would have nothing in common with those patronized by the Encyclopedists and their allies and sympathizers. Hers was a salon that catered exclusively to the nobility and to those poets, painters, and musicians favored by the court and whose works steered clear of controversy and in no way challenged officially approved opinions and standards of taste. Besides, loyalty to her royal patroness precluded any serious contact with authors or artists who might be found objectionable.

For an ambitious, hard-working artist like Vigée Le Brun, a salon was meant to provide pleasant social, literary, and musical diversions, and hardly anything more. Unlike the other eighteenth-century *salonnières*, Vigée Le Brun had little intention of staking her claim to fame as a hostess, let alone as one committed to any cause looked at askance by the monarchy to which she owed everything. Besides, she was both wary of and generally indifferent to the kind of intellectual and philosophical debates that so passionately engaged the minds of so many men and women of her time. As for the rich aesthetic and often contradictory currents that characterized contemporary painting—from the pleasingly and slyly rococo style of Boucher or Fragonard to the austere neoclassical revival advocated by Vien or the promising young David—Vigée Le Brun tended to be eclectic and was intuitively susceptible to those trends that appealed to her sensibility as an artist and that she could seamlessly incorporate in her own paintings (fig. 6).[6]

The concerts that Vigée Le Brun organized in particular attracted great lords and ladies as well as personalities from the conservative circles of the arts and letters. In this respect, her salon was more of a throwback to the seventeenth century and the reign of the all-powerful Louis XIV; it was something of an anomaly in the Age of Enlightenment and the crisis-ridden reign of the ineffectual Louis XVI, when all leading *salonnières* had severed any dependence on the court and did not hesitate to cater to celebrities that had made a name for themselves by boldly challenging the political and social status quo.[7] By strictly limiting her guests to officially sanctioned writers and musicians—and especially to those favored by Marie-Antoinette—Vigée Le Brun hoped to avoid

FIG. 6. *Elisabeth Vigée Le Brun*, Bacchante, *1785. Musée Nissim Camondo, Paris.*
(Photo: Laurent-Sully JAULMES. All Rights Reserved)

any risk of displeasing the court and to ward off any cause for criticism or embarrassment.

Interestingly, however, in spite of her unquestioned loyalty to Versailles, Vigée Le Brun did not completely turn her back on the forward-looking writers and artists of her time. Her father, after all, had belonged to a circle of friends also frequented by such artists as Greuze and Vernet, and even by Diderot and d'Alembert of *Encyclopédie* fame. She could hardly ignore the fact that both Greuze and Vernet, who generously encouraged her first efforts as a painter, were among Diderot's favorite artists, as the enthusiastic praise he lavished on them in his *Salons* amply attest. Greuze, in particular, who endeavored in his frequently melodramatic compositions to enact Diderot's program of a new, morally uplifting art extolling what we would today call family values, would remain a steadfast friend of Vigée Le Brun and admirer of her work. Indeed, he recommended her to his Russian patrons after her flight from Paris in 1789, signed a petition to allow her back to France, and was her first visitor when she returned to Paris in 1802 after her long exile.[8]

Even more interestingly, Vigée Le Brun remained a reader and admirer of Rousseau, hardly an idol of the court. She did not seem concerned with this apparent contradiction, for like many other members of her generation, especially women in search of meaningful self-fulfillment, she found in him a kindred soul, a relationship which would intensify after the Revolution and would force her to emigrate and to experience the kind of rootlessness and alienation so eloquently described in his more personal works, notably the *Confessions*. Indeed, if toward the end of her long and eventful life Vigée Le Brun would muster the courage to set down her personal recollections and reveal feelings of a frequently intimate nature, it would be largely due to his example.[9] In this respect she was not unlike other émigrés and Royalists who rejected

Rousseau's radical political doctrine but identified with the romantic dreamer and wanderer. But then, Rousseau had the unique ability of being either revered or execrated for subjective rather than ideological reasons. Furthermore, like other notable women such as Madame de Staël and Madame Roland, who proclaimed themselves disciples of Rousseau, she did not seem to be conscious of the blatant contradiction between his restrictive vision of womanhood—limited to home and hearth—and her own all-consuming ambition as an artist.

Like the Jean-Jacques of the *Confessions*, Vigée Le Brun was keenly aware that, from the outset of her career, she had aroused a great deal of hostility in some people. This doubtless caused her distress and anxiety, although, unlike Rousseau, she was not inclined to dwell on feelings of victimization. Rather, her sunny, cheerful, unpretentious nature, her zest for living, her keen sense of humor, her uncanny ability to see the positive side, and her extraordinary resourcefulness and total self-reliance made her view the events of her life with a healthy, pragmatic realism, although she would be quite candid about some of her personal disappointments, notably her spendthrift, philandering husband (I, 53–54, 92–93) and her pretty but lightheaded daughter (II, 155). One would seek in vain in her *Souvenirs* the tortured quest for self-identity, the recurrent feelings of guilt and remorse, the sense of persecution verging on paranoia characteristic of the *Confessions*. While she felt that a personal memoir need not be confessional and tell-all, she paid homage to Rousseau by citing this revealing thought as an epigraph to her own autobiography: "Writing down my recollections, I shall remember times past, which will thus enhance twofold, so to speak, my existence."

Shortly before the Revolution Vigée Le Brun made it a point to visit Ermenonville, the park and château near Paris where, while a guest of the Marquis de Girardin, Rousseau had died on July 2, 1778, four days before his sixty-sixth birthday (I, 119). He had been buried in a tomb on the Ile des Peupliers (Poplar Island) in the park of Ermenonville, which by the time Vigée Le Brun made her pilgrimage had become a popular and even fashionable destination for throngs of Rousseau fans from all walks of life. Indeed, its very celebrity largely spoiled its charm for her, for, as she recalled in *Souvenirs,* at every step of the way one had to jostle with other visitors (I, 119).

It is indeed ironic and also quite revealing that Rousseau's vogue had grown into such a widespread cult that even Marie-Antoinette visited Ermenonville, accompanied by a whole retinue of courtiers.[10] That this elegant entourage, which would come to symbolize everything that was corrupt under the Old Regime, duly paused in silence before Jean-Jacques' simple tomb in its melancholy and pastoral setting must have indeed offered a rather curious spectacle.

Rousseau's body would not be allowed to rest permanently on this quiet, isolated small island, a place so in keeping with his own love of nature and of solitude. On October 9, 1794, the Convention would order it transferred to the Panthéon, the former church of Sainte Geneviève, recently converted by the authorities into a secular edifice destined to receive the mortal remains of great Frenchmen.

Thanks largely to Rousseau's influence, sensibility—to the point of excessive, lachrymose sentimentality—pervaded manners and mores. The Rousseauan and romantic ideal of a plain, rustic, unadorned way of life even infiltrated Marie-Antoinette's court. Naturalness and simplicity were the order of the day, affecting even women's fashion. So were family values, and Vigée Le Brun's 1787 portrait *Marie-Antoinette and Her Children* is a highly successful iconographic representation of the queen (see plate 11). In this work Vigée Le Brun portrays her not as she had done in her other portraits—as an ethereal, nymphlike young woman dressed in an unadorned white muslin gown—but as an imposing, matronly figure embodying motherhood in its most sacred guise, that of procreator of the Children of France. The composition was meant to project an image reminiscent of the Christian iconographic tradition of the Holy Family and to help overcome Marie-Antoinette's tarnished, indeed increasingly lurid, reputation as an amoral being, entirely dedicated to pleasure and gratification in all their manifestations, especially sexual voluptuousness and sensuality.

Marie-Antoinette and Her Children can indeed be viewed as a Royalist version of the kind of sentimental bourgeois composition that Greuze had perfected with great success in such compositions as *The Beloved Mother,* representing a buxom mother rapturously surrounded by her large and clinging brood, a work which had been enthusiastically praised by Diderot, not merely for its pictorial qualities but especially for its socially useful message: "This is excellent both for the talent it demonstrates and for the moral content it conveys; it preaches population, and depicts most sympathetically the happiness and inestimable advantages deriving from domestic harmony; it says to any man endowed with a soul and good sense: support your family in comfort, make children with your wife, make as many as you can, but only with her, and you can be sure to find contentment at home."[11]

Enlightenment philosophes, in an effort to combat infant mortality and a drop in population, had urged mothers to rear their children at home and denounced the practice of placing them with wet nurses, typically rustic country women who breast-fed other women's infants. Rousseau's *Emile*, first published in 1762, was of course the most celebrated and popular work that advocated family values and the proper way of rearing children. Even upper-class women were encouraged to nurse their own offspring and to avoid entrusting them to mercenaries. Marie-Antoinette herself, doubtless in order to demonstrate publicly the seriousness of her commitment as a mother, made a brave if brief attempt at breast-feeding.[12]

It was especially in her 1787 and 1789 self-portraits (both at the

Louvre) with her daughter, Julie, that Vigée Le Brun gave full pictorial expression to the Rousseauan and Greuzian sentimentalized notion of the good mother, but without the bourgeois moralistic connotations so dear to Diderot. In both paintings a beautiful young mother is portrayed seated, facing the onlooker with a gentle smile of contentment and enfolding her child in a tender embrace, reminiscent of the Madonna and Child icon. In the 1789 *Self-Portrait with Daughter Julie* the focus is on a neoclassical simplicity of composition and dress (plate 12). A youthful and lovely Vigée Le Brun, wearing a loose-fitting white garment that enticingly reveals her right shoulder and arm, and adorned with a reddish shawl, enfolds in her arms little Julie. Vigée Le Brun's self-portraits with her daughter extol the joy of motherhood, but not without a subtle narcissistic touch consisting of emphasizing her own good looks.

It was Vigée Le Brun's Rousseauan taste for simplicity in dress that enabled her to persuade her aristocratic subjects, and even the queen, to pose for her in unadorned, free-flowing white muslin and without elaborate hair styles. But such an informal outfit, deemed by a number of critics as unsuitable for a monarch, led to further trouble for the unpopular queen, as exemplified by the 1783 portrait known as *Marie-Antoinette "en gaulle"* (see plate 8). If by representing her royal subject either as a modestly dressed young woman or as a devoted mother Vigée Le Brun was attempting to redeem the already widely vilified queen by representing her in her universal humanity and her appealing, vulnerable femininity, she did not succeed in helping to stave off the mounting chorus of criticism. By that time Marie-Antoinette's scandalous reputation for extravagance and pleasure, sexual or otherwise, was beyond repair.[13]

But even self-indulgent Versailles could not resist the appeal of the kind of simple, innocent way of life so lyrically depicted in Rousseau's immensely popular novel *Julie, ou La Nouvelle Héloïse*. Marie-Antoinette sought to find pastoral tranquillity and a measure of privacy in a natural setting reminiscent of the sylvan Eden at Clarens, where Julie and Saint-

Preux had exchanged their first kiss. This would be her beloved new *jardin anglais*, which adorned the Petit Trianon, the small palace in Versailles. Unlike Le Nôtre's vast, geometric layouts characteristic of the grand, majestic park surrounding the palace of Versailles, the *jardin anglais* at the Petit Trianon reflected the informal, natural English style of gardening. It is no coincidence that Marie-Antoinette's *jardin anglais* was largely the conception of the painter and landscape architect Hubert Robert, friend and mentor of Vigée Le Brun, who had made a name for himself as the creator of a new kind of romantic landscape, enhanced with picturesque ruins of ancient temples and monuments.[14]

Like most contemporary French painters, Robert had studied in Rome, a stay that had a profound influence on his art. After his 1765 return to Paris, he not only enjoyed great success with his landscapes, which were admired by such discriminating and demanding art critics as Diderot, but also became quite fashionable in the most exalted social circles. Robert's closeness to Vigée Le Brun is also attested to by her 1788 portrait of the artist (see plate 2), one of her most inspired, vigorous, and spontaneous representations of a male subject, which has justifiably been deemed a masterpiece of portraiture.[15] Robert is shown seated, informally dressed in a jacket with open collar, a white scarf loosely tied around his neck. He holds a palette and brushes in his left hand, while his right hand is lightly resting on a rough-hewn table. His head, slightly turned to the left, is covered with thinning gray hair that reveals a large forehead. But what is striking about this portrait is the sitter's extraordinarily lively, animated expression. It is as if we had caught the artist at a moment of creative inspiration.

Not content with her Petit Trianon and her *jardin anglais*, Marie-Antoinette had a model village or hamlet built, including cottages with thatched roofs, a dairy farm, a mill, and a dovecote, also largely designed by Hubert Robert, which would complete her rustic retreat from the formalities and pressures of Versailles. Word soon spread that not only did she dress up as a shepherdess in a fetching costume of white muslin topped by a large straw hat, but the kind of idealized, alluring shepherdess that Marie-Antoinette enjoyed playacting was strongly reminiscent of the provocatively enticing young women who peopled the pastoral compositions of Boucher and Fragonard, or of such literary précieux and courtly heroines as *L'Astrée*—all of whom, of course, bore not the slightest resemblance to real eighteenth-century peasant women.

Vigée Le Brun's admiration for Rousseau never abated, even after the Revolution had caused the Enlightenment philosophes in general, and Rousseau in particular, to become anathema in the European courts and aristocratic circles that she frequented. When she toured Switzerland on two occasions, in 1807–8, she made a point of seeing all the sites associated with Rousseau's life and works, noting wryly the hostility with which his own compatriots had at first greeted the idea of having a statue in his honor in his native city of Geneva, which, "in spite of its republicanism, does not know anything about equality" (II, 186). Coming from a protégée of Marie-Antoinette, an émigrée, and a fierce and loyal Royalist, this is indeed an unexpected comment. Climbing the hill overlooking the promenade where Genevans had actually fought bitterly to stop the erection of the statue of Jean-Jacques, she further commented, "This great writer is generally detested in Geneva" (II, 186).

By 1808, however, Vigée Le Brun had seen and experienced a great deal. No wonder, therefore, that she would respond with deep feeling to the beauty and serenity of Lake Geneva and its picturesque surroundings. By then she had learned to cherish privacy and solitude and to find spiritual comfort and renewal in communing with nature. No wonder, therefore, that Rousseau's famous novel was very much on her mind when she took a boat trip on the lake in honor of Julie and Saint-Preux, the ill-fated couple that had spent there some of their most blissful hours: "My boat was alone on the lake; the vast silence that surrounded me was troubled only by the light sound of the oars. I fully savored a brilliant and beautiful moon; a few silvery clouds followed it in the sky. The lake was so calm, so transparent that the moon and these lovely clouds reflected in it as in a mirror" (II, 180).

In its lyricism this passage is strongly reminiscent of, and most probably directly derived from, Rousseau's *Reveries of a Solitary Walker.* To be sure, writing was not Vigée Le Brun's principal means of personal expression, and in this respect she could hardly compete with such other notable readers of Rousseau as Byron in *Childe Harold,* or Lamartine in his poem "Le Lac." Yet as an artist she strongly responded to Rousseau's ability to evoke landscapes in a uniquely personal, intimate manner, a lesson that would enrich her own inspiration, for even though she is known primarily as a portraitist, the list of works she appended to her *Souvenirs* includes nearly one hundred landscapes done in pastel (II, 354), an aspect of her prolific output that has generally been overlooked.

Vigée Le Brun was a woman with fairly simple personal needs and tastes. She was well aware of her physical attractiveness, but she did not exploit her good looks merely to advance her career as a painter. The notion of achieving power and influence through sexual intrigues did not appeal to her. Neither was she particularly intent on getting rich. To be sure, she took great pride in the fact that her paintings fetched large sums, and she greatly resented the fact that her husband squandered the handsome fees she earned for her portraits, but this did not plunge her into despair. Her own overriding passion was to paint, and nothing could compare with the special kind of pleasure and gratification she experienced as she stood before her easel, palette and brush in hand, attempting to translate onto the canvas the uniqueness of a human personality.

In *Souvenirs* Vigée Le Brun evokes with great nostalgia the waning years of the Old Regime as a period when "one had the time and inclination to have fun" (I, 80). To be sure, she was not an objective witness of her times. And indeed, in the highly privileged circles to which she had gained access, thanks to her exceptional talent as a portraitist, she could fully savor that special quality of life that has been famously characterized by Talleyrand as *la douceur de vivre* (the sweetness of life).

From the perspective of the bitter and deadly struggles that marked the revolutionary era, Vigée Le Brun deemed genteel and mild the cultural controversies that raged in the salons under the Old Regime. Such, for instance, was the Piccinni-Gluck "war," a quarrel that divided music lovers over the respective merits of the operas of Niccolo Piccinni and those of Christoph Willibald Gluck, the German-born composer and protégé of Marie-Antoinette, who seemed to enjoy her role as patroness of the arts, especially music and the theater.[16] The queen even had a beautiful private theater built on the grounds of Versailles, for she liked to act onstage, one of her controversial activities.

Vigée Le Brun's access to the most exclusive circles of both the aristocratic and cultural worlds enabled her to meet nearly all the celebrities of her time, and in *Souvenirs* she indulges in some name-dropping, probably less in order to impress her readers than out of a melancholy longing for the social and artistic brilliance of those irrevocably bygone days. Thus the aging artist fondly evokes a host of men of letters and painters, composers and musicians, opera singers, actors and actresses, and of course high-born men and women who had peopled and enlivened the shiny world of her youth with their remarkable talent, wit, elegance, and graciousness and who had been ruthlessly dispersed or decimated by the Revolution.

With melancholy nostalgia Vigée Le Brun evokes in *Souvenirs* the refined merriment that characterized her own soirées, and the ease and confidence that prevailed among the guests. A great music lover, she was delighted to feature the most notable instrumentalists and singers of her day in her salon, and since she was herself endowed with a pleasing if untrained singing voice, she would sometimes participate in these musical entertainments (I, 79). Gatherings began around nine in the evening. Not too surprisingly, "politics was never discussed" (I, 82), but guests talked a great deal about literature and exchanged the latest gossip.

Vigée Le Brun was too absorbed in her work and preoccupied with her social obligations as a highly successful court portraitist to pay much attention to the political and social storm that was brewing. The dramatic events of 1789 therefore caught her completely by surprise.

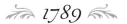

CHAPTER SIX

1789

IN THE MIDST of her very busy life as an exceptionally sought-after and well-connected portraitist, Vigée Le Brun could not help being aware that the brilliant world she so greatly enjoyed was a brittle one. While she seemed to have remained ignorant (perhaps willfully so) of the dire economic realities that oppressed the people, she could not ignore all kinds of ominous rumors that reached her studio or salon.

Unrest was brewing in Paris, and indeed for Vigée Le Brun, who owed everything to the monarchy, the events leading up to 1789 and the ensuing upheaval would forever be etched in her memory as the worst time in her life. Her political allegiance belonged entirely with the court and the aristocracy, who had so consistently shown her great kindness and whom she now came to view as the vulnerable and hapless victims of unruly and bloodthirsty mobs manipulated by ruthless and ambitious political leaders. While her compassion for the poor and downtrodden, whom she consistently tended to identify with unlawful, disorderly, and even criminal members of society, was practically nonexistent, she had immense sympathy for the great and powerful under duress. Indeed in her memoirs she makes it a point to relate the multiple acts of generosity and charity she had witnessed these amiable and gracious people perform in order to come to the aid of the underprivileged. In particular she noted Marie-Antoinette's own benefactions and altruistic impulses, including, for instance, her insistence that her children personally look after little peasants and even, when possible, dine with them and do the honors properly as their hosts (I, 68). She herself had adopted a little village boy named Jacques, supervising his education and providing financially for his family.[1]

Always eager to escape the capital, Vigée Le Brun accepted many invitations to spend a few days at country estates, whether in Louveciennes, where Madame du Barry had retired in the château of Saint-Germain, with its beautiful large park that belonged to the Duke of Noailles, known for his witticisms, or at Malmaison, a château that was then owned by the pretty and fashionable Countess du Moley and that would later be made famous by Empress Josephine as her residence after Napoleon had divorced her. It was during a stay at Malmaison in June 1789 that a dinner conversation contributed to Vigée Le Brun's growing apprehension and made her aware that even in this privileged circle there were ardent partisans of a radical political and social change. These included the Abbé Sieyès, future revolutionary leader, and even Count du Moley himself, who was "vociferously denouncing the nobles," and everyone else "was shouting and speechifying on the best ways to bring about a general upheaval" (I, 131).

Her apprehension and dread mounted in the months preceding the actual outbreak of the Revolution, fed by unmistakable signs of the coming storm. The time for such refined cultural diversions as Greek suppers, operas, comedies, and poetry already seemed to belong to an irretrievable past, abruptly replaced by portents that filled her with dread. Thus it was that at one of her soirées she learned from her guests that the populace had stopped the carriages in which they were taking a ride, clambered onto the steps, and shouted such threats as "Next year you will be behind your carriages and we are the ones who will be inside!" (I, 138).

Around the same time Vigée Le Brun spent a few days at the château of Marly (subsequently destroyed during the Revolution), where
another revealing incident took place. When a drunkard was picked up
in the courtyard, a bunch of leaflets fell from his pockets proclaiming
such slogans as "Down with the royal family! Down with the nobles!
Down with the priests!" (I, 132). Worse still, when local marshals were
summoned to take the man for questioning, a valet who had been in-
structed to follow them reported back that "as soon as they were out
of sight they locked arms with their prisoner and broke into song with
him" (I, 132). Upon learning this Vigée Le Brun was more alarmed than
ever, for what authorities could one rely upon when "the forces of order
made common cause with the guilty?" (I, 133).

Direct threats even reached Vigée Le Brun in her own residence.
The Le Bruns had recently moved to more elegant, spacious quarters
on the rue du Gros-Chenet (presently rue du Sentier), as befitted their
exalted social status. Suspicious-looking characters were seen prowling
about, and when she looked out of her window she would see men whom
she contemptuously refers to in her memoirs as "sans-culottes"[2] making
menacing gestures in her direction with their clenched fists (I, 139).
Doubtless her reputation as the detested Marie-Antoinette's portraitist
had something to do with the fact that she had become the target of
popular hostility, as numerous scurrilous lampoons also made clear.

For a number of years she had toyed with the idea of spending some
time in Rome, hardly a surprising notion, for ever since the Renaissance
an essential part of the cultural education of French painters was to
study and work in the Eternal City. Some artists of the classical period,
notably Nicolas Poussin (1594–1665), had even ended up living there
permanently. Indeed France had (and still has) its own "Académie" in
Rome, a haven for artists created by Louis XIV.

Most of Vigée Le Brun's contemporaries had made the pilgrimage to Rome, notably Boucher, Fragonard, David, and her friends and

mentors Greuze and Hubert Robert. She was aware that a stay in Italy would be greatly beneficial to both her art and her career. But it was her very success as a portraitist and her numerous commissions that had prevented her from making the trip (I, 143). Now, she thought, would be a propitious time to leave France.

The one thing that held her back was the Salon exhibit, scheduled to open at the Louvre on August 25, 1789. The Salon had been her testing ground since she had first exhibited her portraits there in 1783. Paris was in the grip of revolutionary fervor, but artistic life was pursuing its course, and it so happens that her contributions to this particular Salon were of an exceptionally high quality. Her art had deepened and acquired a new seriousness, as is exemplified by her superb 1788 portrait of Hubert Robert (see plate 2), her friend and mentor widely admired for his romantic landscapes with picturesque ruins. Her masterful portrait belongs to a special kind of portraiture, which can also be found in several of her other works. These paintings aim at capturing the subject while in a state of spiritual rapture, as is also exemplified by her striking 1791 portrait of the Italian composer Giovanni Paisiello (see fig. 9), shown while playing the harpsichord. Indeed, the subjects of these need not necessarily be great artists.

Sublimity of expression was not the exclusive characteristic of sitters noted for their creative accomplishments. Thus, Vigée Le Brun could also represent women, especially those endowed with great beauty, in a moment of total self-absorption, with eyes turned upward as if in deep prayer or meditation, as is the case with her 1783 portrait of the notorious Madame Grand (see fig. 4), who in 1802 would marry the deviously successful diplomat and statesman Charles-Maurice de Talleyrand. Other eighteenth-century artists, notably Greuze and Fragonard, excelled at this genre, and more than likely she had learned from them how to dramatize the art of portraiture in this quasi-theatrical fashion.

In 1778, one decade earlier, Vigée Le Brun had painted the portrait of Joseph Vernet (see plate 3), one of her early mentors who excelled in poetic and lyrical landscapes, as well as in seascapes featuring storms and shipwrecks, a genre that greatly appealed to the contemporary predilection for drama and pathos. That Joseph Vernet was one of Diderot's favorite painters is of course hardly surprising.

Joseph Vernet is shown seated and, like in the Hubert Robert portrait, he appears to be caught in the act of painting, with palette and brushes in hand. But unlike Robert, Vernet is shown fashionably dressed, with a frilly lace jabot and cuffs. His demeanor is one of calm, self-contained concentration rather than creative inspiration. It is easy to imagine him just as much at ease in a salon as in his studio. His handsome good looks and aristocratically refined features and genteel, composed expression, as well as elegant attire bespeak the highly successful academician showered with official honors rather than the pre-Romantic artist adept at rendering rugged landscapes and stormy seascapes.

The contrast between the 1778 *Joseph Vernet* and the 1788 *Hubert Robert* is striking. While the *Joseph Vernet* is an uncommonly impressive example of eighteenth-century portraiture, the *Hubert Robert* is a truly original and powerful work. Other portraits Vigée Le Brun exhibited at the Salon of 1789 were those of the ill-fated Dauphin, Louis XVII, who probably died of neglect and malnutrition while imprisoned in the temple, and of the Duchess of Orléans. Her husband, the Duke of Orléans and cousin of Louis XVI, would side with the revolutionaries, vote for the execution of the king but end up himself on the guillotine. Vigée Le Brun's paintings were very well received, but this hardly allayed her fears.

Living in a state of great anxiety affected Vigée Le Brun's physical and mental health. She was afraid to remain in her own home, gradually became unable to work, stopped eating, and lost a considerable amount of weight. Her alarmed friends tried their best to help her, and she accepted temporary refuge with the family of the architect Brongniard, who resided near the Invalides (I, 142). There her hosts did everything they could to calm and reassure her and, since she could not eat solid food, nourished her on broth and wine. But all this solicitude had hardly any effect. She sensed that everything she had achieved was now being threatened and that the kind of genteel, elegant life she loved was coming to an end.

Vigée Le Brun had always been an optimist, supremely confident in her own talent and ability to overcome such obstacles to her success as her gender and professional jealousy. This time, however, she felt overwhelmed by forces beyond her comprehension. Consumed with dire foreboding, she sank into a deep depression and kept repeating these questions: "What is the use of living? Why bother taking care of oneself?" (I, 139). When her well-meaning hosts would take her out for a walk, she would see immense crowds gathered near the Invalides, a sight that only contributed to her sense of dread, for in the teeming Parisians festively assembled to signal their support of the uprising she perceived only ferocious-looking, bloodthirsty ragtag rabble that had nothing in common with "either workers or peasants" (I, 141). She intuitively sensed the underlying violence and pent-up rage in these popular demonstrations and felt, not without reason, that she was one of their targets.

She briefly returned to her home, where she found the whole household in total disarray. For a fortnight she went to live with the Rivière family, to whom she was related by marriage through her younger brother, Etienne, who, thanks to her influence and his own abilities as a poet and playwright in the sophisticated style of Marivaux, had prospered under the Old Regime, rising to positions of prestige, notably that of Secretary to the Comtesse de Provence, sister-in-law of Louis XVI. In 1784 Etienne had married Suzanne Rivière, daughter of Jean-Baptiste Rivière, *chargé d'affaires* in Paris of the Elector of Saxony. Suzanne Vigée was a gifted singer, pianist, and amateur actress who frequently took part in her sister-in-law's soirées. A portrait that Vigée Le Brun painted of her in 1785 (private collection) makes up for the sitter's lack of conventional beauty by highlighting her animated features and intelligent, expressive eyes.

Unlike his sister, Etienne Vigée would side with the revolutionaries but was briefly imprisoned under the Terror, only to be released with the Fall of Robespierre. Obviously Etienne Vigée had the gift for survival and knew how to adapt to rapidly changing political circumstances. When Napoleon came to power he devoted some of his most eloquent verse to singing his praises, and after Waterloo celebrated Louis XVIII in equally fulsome verse, denounced the Revolution, and was duly rewarded with various honorific distinctions. These included the prestigious chair of literature at the Athénée as a successor to Jean-François de La Harpe, former protégé of the philosophes who had turned against them and who, in his famous and monumental *Lycée, ou cours de littérature*, had reverted to classical ideals and conservative social values.

During the summer of 1789 events moved at an accelerated pace. The popular mood was growing increasingly aggressive and violent, with several instances of bloody and arbitrary acts of retribution.[3] Among the newspapers that began appearing at this time the more sensational ones, such as Jean-Paul Marat's vociferous and demagogic *L'Ami du Peuple (The Friend of the People)*, ruthlessly exploited this murderous mood. No one grasped more forcefully than Vigée Le Brun the ominous portent of these developments and the fact that crowds could at a moment's notice turn into ferocious mobs.

On August 4, the National Assembly took drastic measures and abolished most of the feudal privileges of the Old Regime.[4] On October 5, a large crowd of about seven thousand, consisting mainly of determined, militant women, armed with pikes and other weapons, invaded Versailles and forcefully brought the king and queen to Paris.[5] Upon learning of this from Etienne, who had personally witnessed the arrival of the royal couple at the Hôtel de Ville, Vigée Le Brun overcame her nearly catatonic mental and emotional state and decided that it was high time for her to take the road to exile.

That women had played a key role in bringing the royal family back to Paris seems to have gone unnoticed by Vigée Le Brun, who preferred to look upon this defining event as yet another act of violence instigated by a bloodthirsty mob. The French historian Jules Michelet, acknowledging the crucial role women played in the Revolution, puts it succinctly and eloquently: "Men made July 14, women October 5. Men took the royal Bastille, women took royalty itself, placed it in the grip of Paris, that is of the Revolution."[6]

Under these trying circumstances, even painting, Vigée Le Brun's foremost passion, had been left in abeyance, for she was in no state to work. Rejecting lucrative painting commissions and abandoning unfinished portraits, she hastily made arrangements to leave Paris and France in her own carriage, taking along only her daughter, Julie, then nine years old, and the child's governess. On the eve of her departure, her house was invaded by armed national guards who told her in no uncertain terms that she was not to leave her premises. After their departure, however, two of the guards came back, reassured her that they were her neighbors and that they did not wish her ill, and they strongly urged her to leave as soon as possible, but for the sake of safety she should travel not in her own carriage but rather incognito in a public stagecoach, advice she prudently followed, disguised as a poorly dressed working woman, with a coarse kerchief over her head and partly covering her face.

As the stagecoach slowly lumbered its way out of the French capital, Vigée Le Brun, accompanied by her daughter and the governess, was "in a state that cannot be described" (I, 145). Her anxiety was heightened when the stagecoach went through the populous quarter of Saint-Antoine, a well-known teeming seedbed of revolutionaries. But the neighborhood was eerily quiet, and in her autobiography she wryly comments: "Its inhabitants, working people and others had been to Versailles in order to seek the royal family, and the exertion of the trip caused them all to be asleep" (I, 145). Vigée Le Brun's husband and brother had decided to stay in France, but they closely followed her carriage until it reached one of the city's gates, where they parted tearfully.

Vigée Le Brun had taken with her only some linen and the paltry sum of eighty louis she managed to gather at the last minute, leaving behind all the material fruit of her labors, including her jewelry.

As the stagecoach made its way southward, alarming rumors reached its passengers by way of galloping horsemen who would shout at them the latest dire news, that Paris was in flames and that the king and queen had been massacred. In spite of her mother's efforts to reassure her, little Julie was terrified, for she thought that her father had been killed and their house burned to the ground (I, 146). But as the stage-coach kept rolling through the lovely French countryside Vigée Le Brun's spirits gradually lifted. After a much needed stopover of three days in Lyons, she breathed a sigh of relief as she crossed the border, but felt a twinge of remorse at leaving France so joyfully (I, 147).

The sight of Savoy, with its lofty mountains, the summits of which were lost in mist and seemed to reach to the sky, evoked in her a sense of dread, awe, and stunned admiration. Indeed this type of overpowering landscape, so unlike the flat and placid Ile de France, was entirely new to her. Reaching the Alps on her way from Lyons to Turin and wishing to experience more directly and personally all these natural marvels, she insisted on leaving her stagecoach and disregarding the offer of riding on a donkey, climbed Mount Cenis on foot, at least part of the way (I, 148).

Mountains, and more generally the overwhelming rather than pleasing and comforting aspects of nature, had recently become part of a new aesthetic of the pre-Romantic sublime, displacing the classical ideal of harmonious and orderly beauty. Among those writers who had significantly contributed to this change were Rousseau, especially in his *Nouvelle Héloïse,* with its striking descriptions of the powerful effect mountains had on the melancholy Saint-Preux,[7] and Edmund Burke in his treatise on the sublime and beautiful, which Diderot had used extensively in his *Salons* and in elaborating his own theories of art.[8]

Vigée Le Brun may have been politically tone-deaf, but she was closely and intuitively attuned to all the new aesthetic currents of her time. No wonder, therefore, that she should have responded so enthusiastically to the sight of the Alps. Like the hero of Rousseau's novel, a work that had had a profound impact on her sensibilities, she felt the need to be physically close to the forbidding Alpine landscape. Hence her need to clamber on foot the narrow and mountainous paths, bordered by awe-inspiring gorges and precipices.

Her mind and imagination were filled with the new places she would visit, places where urbanity still reigned and the arts were allowed to flourish. Italy, which since the Renaissance had been the artistic home of French painters and which she had longed to visit, now beckoned and was within reach. To be sure, she now assumed the ambiguous and problematic identity of the political exile, perhaps permanently deprived of her homeland. But she would be able to pursue her career in such great cities as Rome, Naples, Berlin, Vienna, and St. Petersburg. She was then thirty-four years of age, and little did she suspect at the time that her exile would indeed be a long one, lasting twelve years, and that when she would at last be allowed to return to France, in 1802, she would find it so profoundly transformed that in effect her expatriation would become a permanent state of personal, spiritual, and artistic estrangement from her motherland.

CHAPTER SEVEN

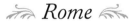 Rome

THE EXPERIENCE of the sublime through the discovery of the Alps was a galvanizing moment for Vigée Le Brun. It snapped her out of her depression and restored her naturally optimistic frame of mind. She now eagerly looked forward to discovering Italy and its rich cultural heritage. After all, had she not long dreamed of seeking a better understanding of the classical sources of art by visiting and even making a prolonged stay in Italy, as was customary for any serious artist?

In 1789 the area that is now known as Italy comprised several small independent kingdoms and duchies which competed for supremacy and were frequently at the mercy of such powerful neighbors as Austria, France, and Spain. Political frontiers and differences in customs and laws separated the Italian kingdoms and duchies. By 1748 Naples, Sicily, and the duchy of Parma had passed to the Spanish Bourbons, and the duchies of Milan, Mantua, Tuscany, and Modena to Austria. Still independent were the Papal States and the declining republics of Venice, Genoa, and Lucca, and the kingdom of Sardinia. The French Revolution would ignite Italian national aspirations.

Arriving in Italy, after all the tribulations encountered in escaping from France, was an immense relief for émigrés like Vigée Le Brun.

On her way to Rome an exhausted Vigée Le Brun stopped off for about six days in Turin, the handsome capital of Piedmont, a city that had become a center of émigrés and counterrevolutionaries. At first unable to find decent lodging in the crowded city, she was obliged to stay in an inadequate inn. She was soon rescued, however, by the engraver Carlo Porporati, whom she had known in Paris. Now a teacher in Turin, he graciously insisted on having her, as well as Julie and the governess, as his guests in his home. Not only did he provide all the comforts and amenities she badly needed after her arduous journey, he also offered to serve as her guide in a city brimming with culture and art.

Vigée Le Brun was not particularly eager to meet other émigrés, even those she had known in Versailles, and so she kept socializing to a minimum. She probably planned on renewing her contacts and reestablishing her clientele in Rome. In the meantime, she would make the most of her brief stay in Turin in order to concentrate on discovering the city and its lovely surroundings. She was especially intent on visiting its art collections, notably its Royal Gallery (of which Porporati would become director in 1797). There she paid particular attention to paintings of the Dutch and Flemish schools in which she had a special interest, which was initially awakened during her 1781 trip to Flanders with her husband, himself a keen connoisseur of Northern art. She singled out several "admirable" portraits by Van Dyck, probably her favorite artist, as well as *The Dropsical Woman* by Gerard Dou, a painter who excelled in depicting scenes and types of everyday life in meticulous and fascinating detail. She did not hesitate to call this delightful composition "a masterpiece in its genre" (I, 150). It is worth noting that *The Dropsical Woman* would be offered to one of Bonaparte's marshals, Count Bertrand Clauzel, who in 1799 forwarded it to the Louvre, where it has been ever since.[1] Ever the obliging host and guide, Porporati also took his guest to the theater, where she recognized, seated in the first loges, the prince Louis-Joseph de Condé and his son, the ill-fated duc d'Enghien (who in 1804 would be kidnapped on German territory, transferred to Vincennes, and shot there on the orders of Bonaparte). Apparently, she made no effort to renew her acquaintance with them (I, 152).

She was impressed by the beauty of Turin, by its rectilinear layout of streets, and its imposing palaces. In this respect, her reaction was not unlike that of other eighteenth-century travelers. Rousseau, for instance, upon arriving in Paris in 1742, deemed it greatly disappointing and far inferior to Turin, for he sought in vain in the French capital the kind of "beauty of the streets and symmetrical alignment of houses" he had admired in the Italian city.[2] As for the Turin inhabitants, obviously Vigée Le Brun did not have enough time to get to know them and is content to report, without comment, that when she asked Porporati whether they were art lovers, his answer made it very clear that he had only disdain for their aesthetic sensibilities (I, 151).

Vigée Le Brun and Porporati became good friends during her stay in Turin, and he would again act as her host when, more than two years later, she would again briefly visit Turin. She painted a portrait of her engaging host's daughter (in Turin's Pinacoteca), which brilliantly succeeds in capturing the young girl's loveliness and which Porporati promptly engraved. In fact, he successfully engraved a number of her portraits, for he had a natural affinity for her style, and he thereby contributed significantly to her fame by making her works more accessible through the medium of print.

Vigée Le Brun left Turin having accomplished her main purpose, which was to do what every serious-minded artist does in Italy and what extraneous circumstances, especially the fact that she was a woman, had prevented her from doing: to complete and enrich her aesthetic education through firsthand exposure to works of antiquity and the Renaissance. Her eagerness to fill this gap in her training also explains her reluctance to squander precious time in socializing. Throughout her stay in Italy she would take advantage of every opportunity to visit every art gallery and private collection. Perhaps subconsciously she could not reconcile herself to the idea of seeing herself as merely an émigrée fleeing from France to save her skin. In this respect, the outbreak of the French Revolution ironically enabled Vigée Le Brun to accomplish a project that had long been dear to her. In this connection it is also worth noting that her estranged husband, who had remained in France but was intent on rehabilitating his wife's reputation, both as an artist and as a good citizen, would attempt to justify her precipitous departure for Italy for the same reasons.[3]

Vigée Le Brun's next stop on the way to Rome was Parma, a small state acquired by the Bourbons of France. There again she found an obliging host and guide in the person of Count Flavigny, minister of Louis XVI, whom she had never personally met in France but who showed her every kindness. With Count Flavigny as her guide, she visited the sites and churches, and spent a great deal of time looking at compositions by Correggio, even climbing, with her usual fearlessness, to the tops of churches for a close-up look at frescoes by this artist (I, 152). During her brief stay in Parma she was elected a member of its Academy on November 3, 1789.

After a brief stopover in Modena, a pretty city that struck her as a pleasant place where one might want to live (I, 153), she arrived in Bologna. There she learned that even though French émigrés were allowed to stay in the city for only one night, she had received the authorization from papal authorities to remain there as long as she wished (I, 154). She promptly visited all the churches and palaces housing masterpieces of Guido Reni, Guercino, Carracci, and Domenichino, among others.

When she arrived in Florence, she put on hold her desire to get to Rome as swiftly as possible in order to explore the treasures of Florentine art. She was of course aware that this was the Florence of the Medicis, and she admired the great works of art that were their legacy, notably the

Chapel of the Medicis, built by Michelangelo. She was equally intent on visiting the famed collections of the Pitti and the Uffizi Palaces. In *Souvenirs* she summarizes her stay in Florence as one of sheer "enchantment" (I, 160). Carriage rides along the Arno River in the evening agreeably complemented the arduous daytime visits to museums and galleries. But the thought of France in the grip of a revolution was always in the back of her mind, and it frequently interfered with her evident satisfaction at this unexpected opportunity of completing her artistic education: "I would have been the happiest of women if I did not have to think of poor France" (I, 161). Perhaps a tinge of nostalgia for her native land already colored her first impressions of Italy.

The highlight of Vigée Le Brun's stay in Florence was probably an invitation to contribute a self-portrait for the Grand Ducal Gallery at the Uffizi, a hardly surprising commission in view of the fact that the Grand Duke was Marie-Antoinette's brother. She was keenly aware that her Uffizi *Self-Portrait* (plate 13) would grant her immortality by ensuring her a place alongside the greatest painters, including Raphael. She was also especially pleased that among the self-portraits of contemporary artists in this collection was one featured by Angelica Kauffmann, a painter she greatly admired as "one of the glories of our sex" (I, 160), and whom she would go out of her way to visit shortly after her arrival in Rome and in whose home she would spend two evenings filled with lengthy conversations (I, 167).

She had been particularly eager to see the self-portrait of Angelica Kauffmann in the Uffizi, for she felt inspired by the thought that her own self-portrait would hang in the same gallery. On a personal level, she also had much in common with this artist, for Kauffmann, like Vigée Le Brun, had been a youthful prodigy whose success had fueled the fires of envy and whose marriage to a charming but unscrupulous libertine had ruined her financially.[4] Vigée Le Brun would pay tribute to her exceptional talent, wit, and "prodigious" erudition, but not without qualifying her compliments with the observation that Kauffmann's conversation, although enormously informative, utterly lacked in enthusiasm (I, 167).

Perhaps for the first time, Vigée Le Brun experienced a certain uneasy sense of inferiority, for she reluctantly admits to her own "limited erudition" in comparison with that of the immensely accomplished and scholarly artist who had frequented the most elite artistic and literary circles in England and Italy and had befriended and painted portraits of such greats as the art historian Winckelmann, the author Goethe, the painter Reynolds, and the actor Garrick.[5] To be sure, like Kauffmann she had proved her mettle by treating allegorical and mythological subjects, and it has been suggested that the neoclassical influence of Kauffmann is present in some of her best portraits, notably that of the notorious *Lady Hamilton as a Sibyl* (1791–92, in an English private collection), which accompanied her throughout her travels in Europe and which she considered a historical painting rather than a mere portrait.[6]

Le Brun's *Self-Portrait*, actually painted in Rome in 1790, is one of her best-known self-representations (see plate 13). It shows her as a young, attractive-looking artist, seated before her easel and confidently facing the onlooker with a slight smile on her lips, her right hand holding a brush about to touch up a canvas, and her left hand grasping a palette and several brushes. Her pleasingly oval face is gently framed by auburn curly hair, and her headgear is a loose kind of white gauze turban. She wears a simple black dress, enhanced by a red belt tied in the back and by a delicately frilly white lace collar that enhances her swanlike neck. That the canvas she is working on represents the chalk outlines of the sketchy but recognizable features of Marie-Antoinette is not only politically significant, for it underscores the artist's recent position as the queen's official portraitist, but it also signifies her continuing loyalty to her royal patroness, in spite of the drastically changed political circumstances. And indeed, Vigée Le Brun's affectionate attachment for the ill-fated queen would never waver throughout the latter's tribulations and final tragic end.

To be sure, the 1790 *Self-Portrait*, like all others by Vigée Le Brun, is not without an element of self-complacent narcissism, and it lacks the psychological insight and depth of self-perception and unvarnished truth we admire in a Rembrandt. One would seek in vain in the serene, smiling features of the lovely young artist so gracefully and self-assuredly poised before her easel even a faint trace of melancholy and suffering reflecting the dread, fear, and emotional turmoil she had so recently experienced as an exile fleeing her native France for her life, and especially as a woman traveling alone in an eighteenth-century Europe besieged by war and revolution. The *Self-Portrait* nevertheless constitutes a proud and courageously optimistic affirmation of the superiority of art over external circumstances. It proclaims Vigée Le Brun's sense of personal and artistic liberation and renewed confidence in her talent, beauty, and youthful vigor and creativity. She had not only survived the greatest crisis in her personal and professional life, she was now poised to face alone the multiple challenges awaiting her in her quest for artistic achievement and recognition beyond the borders of her native country and in the far-flung courts of Europe, and this in a period of shifting allegiances and sudden, unpredictable political changes.

After leaving Florence somewhat reluctantly and with the firm intention of returning later to investigate more fully its cultural riches, Vigée Le Brun arrived in Rome in late November of 1789 and took up temporary residence at the Académie de France, where she was graciously received by its director, the history painter François-Guillaume Ménageot, who harbored Royalist sympathies and was therefore particularly attentive to Vigée Le Brun's needs.[7] He even lent her money she badly needed for her immediate expenses, for her husband had allowed her to leave France with only eighty gold louis, a paltry parting gift in light of the huge fees she had earned as an enormously successful portraitist (I, 163).

For an eighteenth-century artist like Vigée Le Brun, Rome embodied venerated antiquities as well as the very ideal of great classical art, and she had long nurtured the dream of visiting this great city and its artistic treasures. Ironically, it took the revolutionary upheaval to afford her this opportunity of plumbing the riches of the Eternal City. Indeed, as she aptly puts it in her *Souvenirs:* "The satisfaction of living in Rome could alone console me somewhat of the sorrow of having left my country, my family, and so many friends I cherished" (I, 172).

Once more she was the diligent tourist, relying on her vast reserves of energy in order to visit the enormous collections of the Vatican and to explore such famous sites as the Colosseum, the Pantheon, the Capitol, as well as a number of churches and palaces. She was greatly impressed by Michelangelo's frescoes, which she deemed "sublime in composition and execution" (I, 164). The Vatican's Raphaels, on the other hand, moved her more deeply and led her to reflect on the unfairness of the premature death of this genius at the very height of his creative powers. That Raphael was also supposed to have been a dissolute, pleasure-loving libertine whose excesses had contributed to his early demise left her in a pensive, meditative mood, for in her mind such a discrepancy between the man and the artist was indeed baffling and difficult to comprehend: "No," she tried to reassure herself, "one only has to look at his Madonnas to be convinced of the contrary" (I, 165).[8]

Vigée Le Brun's musings on this subject reflect a deep-seated aesthetic preoccupation more fully explored by Diderot in his provocative dialogue, *Rameau's Nephew*, part satire and part character sketch, which relentlessly and brilliantly pursues the theme that a great genius can also be an unscrupulous and egotistical human being capable of wreaking havoc among relatives and friends.[9]

PLATE I. Portrait of Etienne Vigée, Brother of the Artist, *1773*. *Saint Louis Art Museum, St. Louis, Missouri.*

PLATE 2. Portrait of Hubert Robert, *1788. Musée National du Louvre, Paris.*
(Réunion des Musées Nationaux/Art Resource, NY)

PLATE 3. Portrait of Joseph Vernet, *1778. Musée National du Louvre, Paris.*
(Réunion des Musées Nationaux/Art Resource, NY)

PLATE 4. Portrait of Charles-Alexandre de Calonne, *1784*. *Windsor Castle, United Kingdom. (The Royal Collection © 2004, Her Majesty Queen Elizabeth II)*

PLATE 5. Portrait of Madame du Barry, *1782*. *The Corcoran Gallery of Art, Washington, D.C., William A. Clark Collection.*

PLATE 6. Self-Portrait with Cerise Ribbon, *1781. Kimbell Art Museum, Fort Worth, Texas. (In recognition of his service to the Kimbell Art Museum and his role in developing area collectors, the Board of Trustees of the Kimbell Art Foundation has dedicated this work to the memory of Mr. Bertram Newhouse [1883–1982] of New York City. Copyright © 2004 by Kimbell Art Museum)*

PLATE 7. Marie-Antoinette "en robe à paniers," *1778*. *Kunsthistorisches Museum, Vienna, Austria.*

PLATE 8. Marie-Antoinette "en gaulle," *1783. Collection of Princess von Hessen und bei Rhein, Darmstadt, Germany.*

In Rome Vigée Le Brun endeavored to recreate the kind of life she had so greatly enjoyed in prerevolutionary Paris, which combined a demanding schedule of hard work as an artist with relaxing social activities. In 1789 and 1790 Rome was full of French refugees, and Vigée Le Brun quite naturally felt more at ease in their company than in that of the Roman ladies, although she had full access to the most aristocratic circles of the city. It was imperative for her to resume her work as a portraitist, not only to satisfy her artistic urge, but also to meet her pressing financial needs. To paint in an environment so rich with artistic masterpieces was inspiring. But in order to achieve this aim she had to move several times before finding suitable housing.

The main problem in Rome was the noise that constantly disrupted either her sleep or her work, even when she thought she had at last found peace and tranquillity in a small house located on a side street (I, 169). In April 1790 she was elected a member of the Roman Accademia di San Luca. On the whole, her time in Rome was very pleasant and productive, alternating between commissions to paint portraits and visits to famous archaeological sites, museums, and galleries, as well as concertgoing.

She preferred going by herself to the churches, galleries, and palaces where artworks were to be seen so as to avoid having her enjoyment spoiled by idle conversation. She took delight in roaming around in the city and its picturesque surroundings, making numerous sketches, for she believed that no artist could be in Rome without experiencing the need to take crayon in hand (I, 187). In her walks she went out of her way in order to cross Peter's Square, particularly at sunset when the last rays of the sun lingered on Bernini's colonnade, on the obelisk, and on the fountains. Similarly, she often revisited the Colosseum, preferably at dusk, when its arcades took on a reddish-yellow hue sharply contrasting with the deep ultramarine sky (I, 172). Her imagination stirred by this imposing sight, she would wonder what the arena must have been like when it was filled with gladiators facing ferocious beasts, and, always keenly attuned to the currents of contemporary sensibility, would meditate in a manner later made famous by Chateaubriand on the fragility, instability, and evanescence of human endeavors.

Rome greatly heightened Vigée Le Brun's appreciation of what might be called the pleasure and sublimity of ruins, a new aesthetic that had been introduced in France by her friend and mentor Hubert Robert, who had himself found in Rome the principal inspiration of his compositions in which ruins were the main feature.[10] Diderot, who reviewed Robert's paintings in his *Salons*, was moved to formulate a poetics of ruins that eloquently encapsulates Vigée Le Brun's own intuitive response to the remnants of ancient Rome: "The effect of these compositions, good or bad, is to leave you in a state of sweet melancholy. We fix our gaze upon the remains of a triumphal arch, a portico, a pyramid, a temple, a palace, and retreat into ourselves. We anticipate the ravages of time and in our imagination we scatter across the earth the remnants of the buildings we inhabit. In that moment solitude and silence prevail around us. We are the sole survivors of a nation that is no more. Such is the first notion of a poetics of ruins."[11]

The pleasure-loving and purely sensuous rococo, so brilliantly embodied in the compositions of François Boucher and Jean-Honoré Fragonard, was clearly on the wane, and while stern, civic-minded neoclassicism was asserting itself, primarily in the grandly heroic works of Jacques-Louis David, and would inflame the revolutionary generation, the first signs of the Romantic spirit found expression in the picturesque and evocative landscapes of Hubert Robert.

As a Catholic Vigée Le Brun reveled in the pomp and pageantry that Rome constantly offered to its faithful, and she regularly attended Mass in St. Peter's. She made it a point to be on St. Peter's Square on Easter so as to take in the imposing spectacle of the huge square filled with an immense crowd of worshippers dominated by the figure of Pope

Pius VI (a staunch opponent of the French Revolution), dressed in white, raised on a platform, and surrounded by all the cardinals.

She also took a keen interest in the role women played in Roman society, even though her busy schedule and preference for French émigré society prevented her from socializing with them. Always curious to observe her surroundings, however, she noted, for instance, that on Sunday morning women from the lowest classes would appear in droves around the Colosseum and even attend Mass adorned with extravagant ornaments and fake jewelry, and with enormous hoops hanging from their ears. She was told that these women did none of the household chores and lived in total idleness, with the result that poverty forced them into prostitution. She was also intrigued to learn that not only men but also women felt compelled to carry a dagger for self-protection, for violence and murder always lurked in the streets of Rome.

In spite of all the cultural riches Rome offered Vigée Le Brun, after eight months she grew eager to proceed to Naples, where a considerable émigré society had moved and where she would be able to count on a number of commissions for portraits. On April 7, 1790, she left for Naples, which she reached after a two-day voyage through the lovely Italian countryside and during which her daughter Julie, who accompanied her throughout these peregrinations, marveled at the seaside upon seeing it for the first time (I, 195).

CHAPTER EIGHT

⚜ *Naples, Venice, Milan* ⚜

Upon arriving in Naples on April 9, 1790, Vigée Le Brun immediately sensed that it was unique in its attractiveness and a world apart from other Italian cities, Rome in particular. In *Souvenirs* she aptly evokes her first powerful impression of the city: "That brilliant sun, that stretch of sea, those islands perceived in the distance, that Vesuvius from which rose a great column of smoke, and the crowds so animated and noisy and who differ so markedly from those of Rome that one might suppose they were a thousand miles apart" (I, 196). Everything about Naples intrigued and enchanted her.

In the last decade of the eighteenth century Naples was one of the most populous, lively, and colorful cities in Europe. Its population counted nearly half a million inhabitants. It presented a striking mixture of luxury and misery, art and religion. Attracted by the warm climate, numerous aristocratic families, both rich and impoverished, had elected to live there. So did a great number of aspiring artists and a veritable army of men of the cloth.

Naples had become the capital of an independent kingdom ruled by Ferdinand IV, a member of the cadet branch of the Spanish Bourbon line, whose Habsburg consort, Maria Carolina, was a daughter of the formidable Maria Theresa of Austria and therefore a sister of Marie-Antoinette. This was another reason why Vigée Le Brun expected to receive a warm welcome in Naples. And in this she was not disappointed.

Vigée Le Brun had rented a villa at Chiaja on the edge of the sea and directly facing the Isle of Capri, a spectacular location that enchanted her. Soon after her arrival she found herself in the midst of the most exclusive circles of Naples society and busy with numerous commissions for portraits, especially from rich foreign dignitaries able to afford her hefty fees. She was promptly summoned to the court and struck up a friendship with Maria Carolina, who reminded her a great deal of her beloved benefactress Marie-Antoinette and who commissioned her to paint portraits of herself and of her two eldest daughters. Maria Carolina herself was as unpopular with the Neapolitans as Marie-Antoinette was with the French because of her scandalous reputation.

Among Vigée Le Brun's new friends was the immensely wealthy Count Paul Skavronsky, the Russian ambassador to Naples who happened to be her neighbor and therefore invited her to spend many pleasant evenings in the Russian embassy. He was greatly enamored with his lovely wife, a niece of the powerful Russian Prince Grigori Alexandrovich Potemkin, field marshal and famous favorite of Catherine II. Vigée Le Brun was greatly intrigued by the beautiful but indolent Countess Skavronsky, who was the recipient of numerous and extravagant presents from her uncle in the form of enormous diamonds and the latest fashions from Mademoiselle Bertin, Marie-Antoinette's own designer, which she never even bothered to wear (I, 197). What Vigée Le Brun fails to mention in *Souvenirs* is that this unusual generosity might be better understood if one knew that Countess Skavronsky as a young girl had been her uncle's mistress.[1]

Uneducated and probably depressive, Countess Skavronsky would spend her days languidly stretched out on a daybed. Yet Vigée Le Brun found her irresistibly charming in spite of her lethargy and took obvious pleasure in painting her sumptuous portrait of 1790 (Paris, Musée Jacquemart-André). It shows a handsome woman, seated on plush cushions and wearing a rich satin dress, with several strings of pearls adorning her neck and a turban framing her loosely curly hair. Her expression is pleasingly dreamy and vacuous.

As Vigée Le Brun was working on the portrait of Countess Skavronsky she received the visit of William Hamilton, a British diplomat and well known antiquarian and archaeologist, and ambassador to Naples (I, 198).[2] His urgent request was that Vigée Le Brun set every other project aside in order to paint the portrait of the beautiful woman who accompanied him. This woman was his mistress, Emma Hart, to become famous as Lady Hamilton.

Hamilton was a passionate collector of paintings, books, and, from his earlier days in Naples, classical artifacts unearthed during the continuing excavations of Pompeii and Herculaneum begun in 1709, which were to have such important repercussions in art history and literature.[3] He was especially obsessed with Mt. Vesuvius, the volcano that had buried the two Roman cities in A.D. 79, and frequently visited it by day and night, not fearing to observe it close-up despite the perpetual danger of eruptions, gathering numerous lava and rock samples and commissioning paintings of it. Back in England he was made a Knight of the Bath by the king, and his fellow members of the Royal Society affectionately dubbed him the "volcano lover."[4]

Mt. Vesuvius became part of the Grand Tour, and British tourists eagerly visited the volcano as well as the ruins of Pompeii and Herculaneum, seeking great, terrifying experiences. Overwhelming natural phenomena had become part of a new aesthetic of the sublime.[5] The emergence of new modes of perception superseded the rational, orderly, and beautiful, which had embodied the classical ideal, and now stressed the overpowering aspects of nature and their impact on the individual by heightening his awareness of human fragility, vulnerability, and evanescence.

Vigée Le Brun soon discovered that she, too, had succumbed to the fascination of Mt. Vesuvius. The magnificent monster was never free of its threatening smoking plume, and she viewed it as a good omen that her arrival in Naples had been greeted by one of its occasional spectacular outbursts, spewing the most spectacular display of fireworks (I, 209). Mt. Vesuvius was not only her favorite sight in Naples, she soon became obsessed with it to the point of deciding that she had to climb it, an experience she repeated several times, for she was always eager for strong new experiences, no matter how perilous.

The first time she made the climb she and her companions found themselves in the midst of a raging storm and a rain so fierce and thick that it reminded her of the deluge (I, 209). Undeterred, the drenched travelers continued to ascend, with molten lava flowing at their feet. The thunderstorm produced enormous visual and auditory effects, echoing in the surrounding mountains, and the frightful combination of drench and fire struck her as not unlike what it might be like to find herself at the very gates of hell. At last overcome by the smoke and cinders, the travelers got back on their mules and proceeded downward in a rather pitiable state. Far from being deterred by this first rather terrifying experience, she waited only a few days before tackling once more the climb of what she affectionately refers to as her "dear Vesuvius," insisting this time that her daughter be part of the excursion party in order to experience this grandiose spectacle. Although the weather was perfectly serene on this second visit, the volcano put on a good show by spewing so much fire and lava that the earth trembled under the feet of the travelers, to the point of upsetting little Julie (I, 210).

Vigée Le Brun learned more about Sir William Hamilton as she worked on the portrait of his mistress Emma Hart (fig. 7). Hamilton was both an ardent collector and a shrewd dealer who purchased judiciously and resold some of his acquisitions for gratifying sums, notably to the British Museum. Even Vigée Le Brun somewhat maliciously notes in *Souvenirs* that he drove a hard bargain about the fee for the portrait of his mistress and that he eventually resold it in London for a handsome profit (I, 199).

Hamilton's first wife, Catherine, heiress to a considerable estate in Wales, suffered from asthma and was a pious, retiring woman who excelled at the harpsichord. They had been married for sixteen years when she died, leaving him childless. In Naples he had acquired a reputation as an unmatched connoisseur as well as an amiable host, and the best of Naples society vied to attend his elegant gatherings and musical soirées at the British embassy mansion. When Leopold Mozart and his prodigal son visited the city, Catherine somehow managed to overcome her shyness and performed superbly on the harpsichord on that occasion.[6] The refined Catherine was less apt to appreciate her husband's love of hunting, which made him a boon companion to King Ferdinand IV of Naples, a largely uneducated man with rather coarse appetites who enjoyed, above all, going on murderous shooting expeditions.

After his wife's death, Hamilton became hopelessly enamored with the much younger Emma Hart, a gorgeous woman of humble origin, reportedly the daughter of a blacksmith and a servant woman who had migrated to London, where her good looks helped her secure a position as a chambermaid in a solid, respectable family (I, 200). But while in service in this household she devoted so much time to reading novels, an activity greatly frowned upon, especially for young girls, as well as reading plays, an equally reprehensible activity, and even acting out parts in them, that she was dismissed.

Emma Hart's extraordinary talent in assuming dramatic poses and mimicking expressive gestures would eventually serve her in good stead. But in the meantime she found herself without any resources and was probably saved from a life of prostitution and degradation by attracting

FIG. 7. *Elisabeth Vigée Le Brun,* Emma Hart, Future Lady Hamilton, as Ariadne, *1803. Miniature by Henry Bone (copy of Vigée Le Brun's 1790 portrait, in a private collection). Reproduced by kind permission of the trustees of The Wallace Collection, London.*

the attention of rich and aristocratic lovers and of such notable artists as George Romney and even Sir Joshua Reynolds, among others, for whom she modeled for portraits and compositions.

Romney in particular liked to use her as a model for numerous portraits and compositions. One such portrait, executed in 1782, shows her at her most charming and seductive (fig. 8). It was while posing for Romney that she attracted the attention of Lord Charles Greville, a nephew of Sir William Hamilton who fell in love with her but who

FIG. 8. *George Romney,* Portrait of Lady Hamilton, *1782. Copyright The Frick Collection, New York.*

in 1785, finding himself financially ruined, decided to leave for Naples with Emma Hart in tow, probably as a bargaining chip. And indeed his uncle agreed to pay his debts on condition that Emma remain with him. Thus she became Hamilton's acknowledged mistress and an important personality in Naples society, appreciated for her talent as an expressive and strikingly original mimic capable of representing famous historical and legendary characters in what was referred to as *attitudes*. Dressed in Greek or Roman garb she mesmerized her audience, and her talent became widely admired by foreigners visiting Naples, notably Goethe.[7]

In 1791 Hamilton married Emma, thereby making her one of the great ladies of Naples society in spite of her dubious origins, deficient education, poor taste in dress, and deplorable manners. The marriage fared reasonably well, and the unusual couple enjoyed sympathetic notoriety in Naples society until 1798, when Emma Hamilton started her famous love affair with Admiral Viscount Horatio Nelson, an English naval officer who was then stationed in Naples. Nelson would of course go on to become a national English hero in the struggle against Napoleon.

Vigée Le Brun was indeed prescient in remarking that the life of Lady Hamilton constitutes the stuff of novels (I, 199). What she could not predict was that in 1941 a movie titled *Lady Hamilton* would be made and would star the famous and glamorous husband-and-wife team of Laurence Olivier and Vivien Leigh as Admiral Lord Nelson and his flamboyant mistress.[8] Set against the background of the Napoleonic wars, the film focuses on the romance between Lord Nelson and Emma Hamilton, cut short by Nelson's death in 1805 at the Battle of Trafalgar. It was said to have been Winston Churchill's favorite film.[9]

There is no doubt that Emma Hamilton's exceptional beauty, animated physiognomy, and ability to strike dramatic poses held great fascination for Vigée Le Brun as an artist, for she painted several portraits of her in various *attitudes,* notably one as a Persian Sibyl, which must have been one of her favorite paintings, for she carried it with her throughout her European peregrinations. Le Brun did not like Emma personally; she found her common and lacking in style and wit, yet given to disdainful mockery and possessed of considerable craftiness, which enabled her to bring about her spectacular marriage to Lord Hamilton (I, 202).

Vigée Le Brun's first portrait of her was completed in July 1790, when Emma Hart had not yet married Lord Hamilton (see fig. 7). It represents her in a seductively reclining pose, dressed in a flowing, loose gown that exposes her beautiful arms and shoulders, and resting upon a low table adorned with grape leaves and covered by a leopard skin. Her oval, smiling face is framed by long auburn hair flowing down from her bare shoulders to her hips. Her right hand gently supports her face while in her left hand she holds a wine goblet. The background is a mythical kind of grotto with a distant view of the sea dotted by a single vessel. Whether Emma Hart was supposed to represent a bacchante, priestess of love and wine, or Ariadne, the tragic legendary figure of the daughter of Minos betrayed by Theseus, or even a Sibyl, is never made quite clear.[10]

Having learned that Lady Hamilton excelled at the art of taking dramatic attitudes Vigée Le Brun organized a spectacle in her own salon to which were invited all the available notables and aristocrats. The evening was a great success, for Lady Hamilton portrayed so effectively the rapid passage from sorrow to joy, and joy to fear that everyone in the audience was delighted by her performance.

Many years later, however, in 1802, when Vigée Le Brun was in London, she would again meet Lady Hamilton, who had just been widowed. By then she had not only contracted enormous debts as a result of her extravagant living style, but she had also lost her spectacular good looks, grown grossly obese, and reportedly become an alcoholic. Shedding copious tears, she complained that she was greatly to be pitied, having lost in Lord Hamilton not only a spouse but an irreplaceable friend and father, a loss from which she would never recover. Her grief struck Vigée Le Brun as more contrived than real, for, as she recalls in her memoir, "having noticed some music on my piano she began to sing it" (I, 203). Lady Hamilton's end is indeed a sad one, as Vigée Le Brun learned long after having left London. Beset by exorbitant debts, she was imprisoned for insolvency in 1813, and after her release took refuge in Calais, where she died on January 15, 1815, "in isolation and the most abject misery" (I, 204).

While in Naples, however, soon after her marriage and official presentation to the Naples Court, Lady Hamilton managed to get into the good graces of King Ferdinand IV and especially of his consort, Queen Maria Carolina, with whom she enjoyed an intimate relationship. The French Revolution was turning the king against France, and Queen Maria Carolina, elder sister of Marie-Antoinette, not only became unpopular with Neapolitans because of the undue political influence she was exerting, but also because of her reportedly notorious sexual promiscuity with both sexes. Probably because of her own loyalty to Marie-Antoinette, Vigée Le Brun felt a special kinship for the much maligned Queen Maria Carolina, whose portrait she painted, whose looks reminded her of the ill-fated queen of France, and whose moral character she endeavored to defend against her detractors, stressing her qualities of generosity and willingness to bear the main burden of the government because of her husband's inability to assume these responsibilities (I, 226).[11] In this respect, she readily identified with the queen as a woman who, like herself, had found herself obliged to fend for herself in a man's world. The two women established an easy and fairly intimate relationship, especially during the queen's sittings for her portrait.

In spite of her friendly relationship with the Naples Court, Vigée Le Brun tried her best to steer clear of its intrigues, for she was intent on devoting all of her energies to her painting. One of the most remarkable portraits she executed in Naples was that of Giovanni Paisiello, a highly successful and prolific composer whose operas were then being performed at the San Carlo Opera House in Naples (fig. 9). He would be invited by Catherine II to Saint Petersburg and would eventually side with Napoleon, being showered with honors, thanks to the powerful protection of the Emperor, but he ultimately sank into disgrace and poverty in 1815, after Waterloo and the reinstatement of Ferdinand IV as king of Naples.

Vigée Le Brun had attended the premiere of one of Paisiello's operas, *Nina o la paza d'amore*, and began working on his portrait in December 1790. She had recently left her lodging at Chiaja, for even though she loved its picturesque location facing the sea and the Isle of Capri, it was too noisy to allow her to sleep at night. Her new dwelling, closer to Naples, nevertheless had the disadvantage of not being properly heated, and cold spells in December made both the artist and her sitter so uncomfortable that, as she put it in her memoir, she feared she would not be able to complete her portrait (I, 219).

Partially to fend off the cold, Paisiello would compose a piece of music on the clavichord while sitting for his portrait, a circumstance that enabled the artist to seize her subject in a moment of inspiration and improvisation that immeasurably contributes to the exceptional liveliness and dramatic quality of the composition. The musician is represented seated at the clavichord, his hands poised on the keyboard with his nimble fingers caught in mid-action, his still youthful and appealing features suggesting a rapturous ecstasy, his eyes lifted upward, and his lips half-opened as though murmuring to himself the music he was in the act of composing. A sheet of the score of his opera *Nina* that is unfurled in front of his musical instrument is symbolic evidence of his creative genius.

FIG. 9. *Elisabeth Vigée Le Brun*, Portrait of Giovanni Paisiello, *1791*. *Musée National du Château de Versailles, Versailles. (Réunion des Musées Nationaux/ Art Resource, NY)*

The emerging preeminence of the concept of genius coincides with the Enlightenment movement.[12] Since the Renaissance there had been a growing awareness of the role of originality and inspiration in poetry and art, with the emphasis being increasingly placed on individualism. Vigée Le Brun's portrayal of Paisiello captured in that moment of epiphany is therefore entirely in keeping with this new concept of the artist as not merely a person of exceptional talent and accomplished craftsmanship, but as a singularly gifted individual capable of experiencing and of rendering in his works the most profound and universal human emotions. As a musical genius Paisiello embodies in his portrait the main features that the Enlightenment associated with artistic creativity: enthusiasm, inspiration, and originality.[13]

The painting was shipped off to Paris to be part of the 1791 Salon. It is worth noting that Vigée Le Brun was sufficiently pleased with her portrait of Paisiello to submit it to the judgment of her colleagues at the French Académie and the Parisian public, probably in order to remind them pointedly of her existence and accomplishments as a Frenchwoman forced into exile who was managing not only to survive but also to thrive as an artist. In spite of her controversial status as an émigrée she received enthusiastic notices, and even Jacques-Louis David, who had at one time frequented her salon but with whom she had had a strained relationship which was hardly improved by their profound ideological differences, is supposed to have paused at great length in front of her portrait and paid it the supreme compliment of remarking that it could have been painted by a man, at least according to the testimony of her husband, who overheard the laudatory comment and reported it back to her (II, 249). Even though Vigée Le Brun acknowledges that David always recognized her superior talent, she never forgave him for his fierce revolutionary politics as a member of the Convention who voted for the king's death and who campaigned to abolish the Académie Royale de Peinture et Sculpture "as the last refuge of aristocracies" (II, 250).[14]

The Salon of 1791 was the first one held after the outbreak of the Revolution. It was now open to all artists, rather than exclusively to the members of the Académie Royale de Peinture et Sculpture, originally founded in 1648 by Mazarin. The Salon of 1791 was clearly dominated by Jacques-Louis David, the artist who in his neoclassical compositions extolled heroism, civic virtue, and self-sacrifice. Here he re-exhibited, to great acclaim, some of his most celebrated paintings first shown in the Salons of the 1780s, notably *The Oath of the Horatii* (Paris, Musée National du Louvre), viewed as a revolutionary manifesto and, according to a noted David scholar, as "a culmination of the century's desire for moral sublimity and aesthetic simplicity,"[15] as well as his *Brutus Receiving the Bodies of His Sons* (Paris, Musée National du Louvre), yet another picture that came to be closely linked with the revolutionary ideology, and *The Death of Socrates* (New York, Metropolitan Museum of Art), which extols the Stoic nobility of voluntary death.[16] If Vigée Le Brun managed to make her presence felt at the Salon of 1791 it paled in comparison with David's artistic and political triumph as the painter whose works best coincided with the new revolutionary ideal of civic duty and heroism. The Salon of 1791 also enabled Vigée Le Brun's old competitor and rival at the Académie, Adélaïde Labille-Guiard, who had opted to stay in Paris and side with the revolutionary cause, to assert herself. Before 1789 Labille-Guiard had been overshadowed by the glamorous portraitist of Marie-Antoinette. Now she came into her own with no fewer than eight portraits of the new celebrities, notably deputies of the National Assembly.[17] However, poor health, combined with the unpredictable vagaries of revolutionary politics, would prevent her from sustaining her initial success.[18]

Vigée Le Brun loved to discover new landscapes, and Italian cities, with their splendid surroundings, offered her many opportunities for such outings, which she invariably undertook armed with her sketchbook. While portraiture was her official genre as a painter and provided her with a very handsome source of income, the numerous exquisite drawings and pastels she executed throughout her lifetime testify to her keen sensitivity to nature. Probably for financial reasons she never attempted to venture into painting landscapes in oil, a genre that was far less profitable than portraiture, but she greatly enjoyed drawing or doing pastels of natural settings of particular beauty for her own personal satisfaction, and these are indeed among her most intimate and delightful works.[19] Her friends and mentors Joseph Vernet and Hubert Robert, as great landscapists, must have also contributed significantly to developing this aspect of her aesthetic sensibilities. Nor should her reading of Rousseau be overlooked as a major influence in shaping her pre-Romantic responsiveness to nature.

The excursions Vigée Le Brun undertook while in Naples produced several studies of Mt. Vesuvius, as well as of the lovely surroundings of the city.[20] One of her great pleasures was to take long walks along the spectacular seashore in nearby Posollipo, frequently in the company of her daughter, Julie. They would both sit in silence until moonrise, "enjoying the fresh air and the superb view" (I, 220).

Vigée Le Brun had not forgotten the message of Rousseau's *Emile* and the importance of raising a child properly. She therefore endeavored to give her daughter a good education, in spite of the disruptions and frequent displacements caused by her emigration. But the program of study she designed for Julie turned out to be far more ambitious than the one Rousseau had outlined in Book V of *Emile*, devoted to the education of Sophie, the future companion of Emile. In this respect she seems to have subconsciously rebelled against Rousseau's view of women as men's intellectual inferiors.[21] While in Naples she hired masters of writing, geography, music, as well as Italian, English, and German (I, 220). German was the little girl's favorite language, and she also showed some aptitude for painting; but her favorite activity turned out to be writing stories of her own invention. Returning home from one of her evening outings, Vigée Le Brun would find her daughter with pen in hand, and even after sending her to bed she would sometimes catch her in the middle of the night surreptitiously working on one of her little romances. We don't know whether Julie had a real literary talent or indeed whether she was ever encouraged by her mother to cultivate and develop this particular interest, although one of her tales is singled out in the *Souvenirs* for its "situations and style" (I, 221).

In the meantime, Vigée Le Brun was determined to complete her Grand Tour of Italy, and she made her way northward through Spoleto, Florence, Siena, Parma, Venice, Verona, and Turin, which she reached in early August 1792. She had been in Florence before, but only in passing, and while she was pleased to see once more its famed artistic treasures, she was especially impressed by her visit to the Cabinet of Physics and Natural History, directed by Felice Fontana, a distinguished anatomist who had made a name for himself throughout Europe for his wax models of the human body, which were on exhibit for scientific instruction as well as for the perusal of foreign visitors.[22]

Vigée Le Brun curiously examined a number of remarkably accurate and realistic anatomical wax reproductions of various human organs. But what especially stunned her was a life-size wax figure of a human female lying on her back and whose inner organs could be viewed by lifting a detachable cover over her stomach. When Fontana proceeded to do this for the benefit of his visitor, she nearly fainted; for several days afterward she was so obsessed with this sight that she could not look at anyone without mentally stripping this person of his or her clothes and skin (I, 238). When she consulted Fontana about the nervous and depressive state of prostration in which this experience had left her, he reassured her by saying that her unusual sensitivity was part and parcel of her artistic gift: "What you consider a weakness and a misfortune are your strength and your talent" (I, 238). However, she promptly disregarded his rather condescending and flippant counsel, which was that if she wished to rid herself of "the inconveniences of this susceptibility" she should stop painting altogether. If she found this recommendation unthinkable it was for a simple but fundamental reason: "Painting and living have always been one and the same thing for me" (I, 238). She was indeed thankful to Providence for having granted her this talent and chided herself for having foolishly confided to Fontana, who may have known a great deal about human anatomy but not enough about the more mysterious process of artistic creativity, especially when it happened to manifest itself in a woman, to be in a position to offer her thoughtful and helpful advice.

Vigée Le Brun was especially eager to see Venice, where she arrived on the eve of the Feast of Ascension 1792 (forty days after Easter). It so happens that every year a spectacular ceremony (which lasted until 1797), known as *The Festivals of the Doge*, celebrated on this occasion the symbolic marriage of Venice and the sea, the mastery of which was supposed to signify continued prosperity for the city. The Grand Canal was filled with a multitude of gondolas surrounding the *Bucentaur*, an enormous and gorgeously decorated barge carrying the Doge. The marriage was enacted when the Doge threw a gold ring into the sea. Cannon shots announced to the city and its surroundings the consummation of this great wedding, which concluded with a solemn Mass attended by a huge and enthusiastic crowd, and in the evening with other popular and colorful events, such as a contest of skill between gondoliers struggling to throw one another into the sea with their poles, and a final display of spectacular fireworks over the Piazza San Marco. Vigée Le Brun had the privilege of witnessing in person grandiose state occasions masterfully recorded by such painters as Guardi and Canaletto.

Venice has always held a particularly special kind of fascination for writers and artists. In the eighteenth century it offered numerous attractions and enormous cultural riches to visitors like Vigée Le Brun. She fully savored its unique topographical location between sea and sky, and its warm, luminous light, and like generations of visitors before and after her she found a ride along its meandering Grand Canal, bordered by palazzi, churches, and piazzas, a most memorable experience.[23]

As was her practice whenever she arrived in a new city, Vigée Le Brun was impatient to see everything and to learn as much as possible about its history, customs, culture, and art. In Venice she was fortunate in having as her attentive and knowledgeable *cicerone* and guide Dominique-Vivant Denon, whom she had met in Paris and who graciously put himself entirely at her disposal (I, 245).[24] Among the great works of art he showed her she singled out for special admiration twelve portraits in pastel by Rosalba Carriera (1675–1757), a female Italian painter who had been among the first to explore fully the expressive possibilities of this relatively new medium and who had also achieved the rare distinction of being elected to the French Académie Royale de Peinture in 1720. Vigée Le Brun's particular interest in Carriera is understandable in light of what they had in common as successful women artists and as innovative portraitists. The qualities in Carriera's portraits that especially struck Vigée Le Brun were their freshness of color and their psychological truthfulness: "A single one would suffice to make a painter famous" (I, 247).[25]

Denon's variegated career spans the Old Regime and the Napoleonic era and testifies to his remarkable resourcefulness and capacity for surviving and even thriving in a period fraught with unpredictable political upheavals. Born in 1747 into the small French nobility, he came to Paris in 1769 with the intention, like so many ambitious young men from the provinces, of making his mark in the French capital. His initial goal was to become an engraver, and he soon succeeded in attracting the attention of Louis XV, who entrusted him with the directorship of the "Cabinet des Médailles" (part of the Crown's patrimony established by Louis XIV). He also had unusual diplomatic skills, which were acknowledged when he was appointed embassy secretary to Saint

Petersburg in 1774, and following that he was sent on another mission to Switzerland in 1775, where he introduced himself to Voltaire, succeeded in charming him, and drew several portraits of the philosophe.[26] In 1787 he managed to get himself elected to membership of the Académie Royale, and he soon thereafter returned to Italy. He also had strong literary aspirations, and in 1777 he published a scandalously libertine novel titled *Point de lendemain (No Tomorrow)*, an elegantly rococo and cynical tale of sexual seduction and betrayal now recognized as one of the masterworks of the genre.[27]

Denon's brilliant career was to continue unabated during and after the Revolution. After learning that his presence in Italy caused him to be listed as an émigré, he hastened back to France and convinced the painter David that he sided with the revolutionary cause and got himself stricken off the list of émigrés. He even met Robespierre, who promptly appointed him to the post of "National Engraver," with a generous allowance that permitted him to live safely and comfortably during the dangerous and difficult revolutionary years. In 1797 he met the young general Bonaparte at a ball given by Talleyrand, the French statesman and diplomat who was equally adept at surviving in tumultuous times. Denon and Bonaparte engaged in an amiable conversation, and the engraver gained the general's friendship and confidence. A year later he took part in Bonaparte's Egyptian campaign, and in 1803 he was appointed Director of Museums. In this capacity he was instrumental in acquiring for the Louvre numerous masterpieces as spoils of conquest and also designed the Vendôme Column. Even after Waterloo Louis XVIII kept him in his position as Director of Museums. But he refused to accede to the demand of the allies that works of art requisitioned by the French during Napoleon's campaigns be restituted to their original owners. Faced with Louis XVIII's insistence that he comply with this request, he resigned, retiring to an apartment on the Quai Voltaire in

Paris, where he devoted himself to writing an account of his life, career, and travels, as well as to a history of art. He died there in 1825.

Vigée Le Brun did not find Denon physically attractive but was promptly won over by his amiability and vast artistic knowledge. She was also hardly surprised to learn that women found him irresistible. He introduced to her his mistress, the vivacious Isabella Marini, a cultured and emancipated young woman who hosted one of Venice's best-known salons, later frequented by such leading literary personalities of the Romantic era as Germaine de Staël, Chateaubriand, Stendhal, and even Byron. The two women became quite friendly, and Vigée Le Brun painted a delightful portrait of her for Denon. The work highlights her lovely youthful oval face with large, expressive eyes and full, smiling lips, pleasingly framed by abundant, curly black hair casually cascading down to her well-rounded shoulders (fig. 10).

Always a music lover, Vigée Le Brun keenly appreciated the concerts and operas she attended in Venice. Italian music, with its melodic emphasis, was a revelation to her, as it had been to Jean-Jacques Rousseau during his own stay in Venice fifty years earlier, in 1743–44, as secretary of the French ambassador to Venice, Count Montaigu. By an interesting coincidence, both were sent into rapture by the church choir of young girls who remained invisible behind grilled balconies. In *Souvenirs* Vigée Le Brun asserts that nothing she ever heard before or since compared with the simple and harmonious songs executed by these young girls "so that the music seemed to come from heaven and to be sung by angels" (I, 248). Rousseau records having experienced a similar reaction in his *Confessions*, but adds that he felt utterly frustrated by the fact that he was prevented by the screens from seeing the "angels of beauty" who produced these celestial sounds.[28]

Vigée Le Brun loved everything about Venice, but her pleasant stay there was partially marred when she learned that, following Bonaparte's

FIG. 10. *Elisabeth Vigée Le Brun*, Portrait of Isabella Marini, *1792. Toledo Museum of Art, Ohio. (Purchased with funds from the Libbey Endowment, Gift of Edward Drummond Libbey, 1950.243)*

invasion of Italy in 1796, she could never recuperate an investment of thirty-five thousand francs she had made in a Venetian bank; against the advice of friends she neglected to withdraw her funds at the right time, and the money was gone forever (I, 250).

In light of current events in revolutionary France, Vigée Le Brun had to repress her homesickness and reluctantly give up the cherished notion of returning to Paris in the foreseeable future. She also grew increasingly alarmed about the fate of her mother, brother, estranged husband, and friends she had left behind. Her close association with the royal family, whose own situation after the ill-fated flight to Varennes on June 20–21, 1792, followed by its forced return to Paris on June 25, had become increasingly precarious, clearly marked her as an enemy of the revolutionary cause. On August 10, 1792, the storming of the Tuileries Palace forced the Royal family to seek refuge in the Assembly. On February 9, 1792, a decree had authorized the confiscation of property belonging to émigrés, and her name was added to that list, in spite of her husband's repeated petitions to have it removed, claiming in vain that her travels were merely motivated by a desire to perfect her art.[29] In November 1793, at the height of the Terror, Le Brun was even arrested and briefly imprisoned. In December of the same year, her brother Etienne was also incarcerated until July of 1794, after the arrest and execution of Robespierre and his followers marked the beginning of the end of Terror. Furthermore, her husband was in dire financial straits, for he found himself unable to make any sales of works of art in this time of crisis, as his clientele of aristocrats had evaporated since the Revolution. Eventually Le Brun would feel compelled, in order to avoid further personal persecution and to attempt to save the family property, to request the dissolution of his marriage on the ground of desertion. The final divorce decree was issued on June 3, 1794.

Having reluctantly decided to prolong her stay in Italy, Vigée Le

Brun made brief visits to Verona, Turin, and Milan. In Turin she rented a small villa on a hill overlooking the river Po. In this relative solitude, surrounded by lush vineyards and fig trees, she recovered a measure of emotional serenity by socializing with simple, good-natured, and pious peasants who offered a refreshing change from the usual demanding dealings with members of the aristocracy. In this respect, she doubtless had not forgotten Rousseau's exaltation of the virtues of ordinary folks. Their calmness and piety were indeed balm to her agitated state of mind, and as she recalls in her autobiography they "rejoiced the heart and consoled the mind" (I, 260).

Rousseau's spiritual message was not forgotten either, in her belief that religious sentiment is best experienced in a quiet pastoral setting and in small country chapels rather than in magnificent cathedrals and churches: "If I did not attend mass regularly in France, it was not on account of irreligion: but in the churches of Paris, where there is a crowd, I don't feel close to God" (I, 260). This is precisely the kind of religious faith advocated by Rousseau in his famous "Profession of Faith of a Savoyard Vicar," in Book IV of his *Emile*. It is only in the silence of solitude that one can listen to the inner voice of one's conscience and sense the presence of God through a profound communion with the beauty and harmony of nature.

Milan would be Vigée Le Brun's last stopover in Italy, and she was gratified by the warm reception that greeted her. On the day of her arrival she was serenaded under her windows as an inducement to prolong her stay in the city (I, 261). She attended opera performances at the Scala, visited art galleries, and was especially moved by Leonardo da Vinci's *Last Supper*, in what used to be a refectory of the Church of Santa Maria delle Grazie. She acknowledged it as "one of the masterpieces of the Italian school," but, while admiring the figure of Christ, so nobly represented, and all the other characters, painted with such expressive truthfulness, she deplored its damaged state, adding, however, that if one looked at the composition from a certain distance, "it still produced an admirable effect," and that one could imagine what it was like in its pristine state (I, 262). In *Souvenirs* she reports that she later learned that further damage was caused by Bonaparte's soldiers, who amused themselves by taking shots at the *Last Supper*. "A curse on these barbarians!" was her indignant comment (I, 262).

Following her custom, she made extensive excursions beyond the city, enjoying its spectacular surroundings, notably Lake Maggiore, famous for its beauty and varied landscape, and its two islands, *Isola Bella* and *Isola Madre*. On the whole, however, Milan tended to remind her of Paris because of the sophistication and elegance of its society and its ostentatious luxury. She also sensed that there was less than a welcoming attitude in Italy toward the increasing influx of political émigrés from France.

The Austrian ambassador, Count Johann Wilczek, took a personal interest in Vigée Le Brun and urged her to move to Vienna, where, he assured her, she would be very warmly received and where there would be very promising prospects for her as a painter and portraitist because of her close royal connections, especially with Marie-Antoinette, who after all was the daughter of Maria Theresa, the powerful empress of Austria. After three years in Italy during which she had restlessly moved from city to city, she felt she had practically exhausted the treasures of Italian art, and, no longer expecting anything from her homeland, she decided to heed the Austrian ambassador's advice in the hopes of finding in Vienna some kind of personal stability and financial security.

At the last concert she attended in Milan she made the acquaintance of an attractive Polish noblewoman, Countess Bistri, and struck up a friendship with her and her husband. And since they, too, happened to be about to leave for Vienna, they decided to travel together. They made the long journey from Milan to Vienna, admiring on the way the picturesque and at times grandiose Tyrolean and Styrian landscape dotted by mountains, waterfalls, and medieval castles. Vigée Le Brun eagerly looked forward to discovering a new social and cultural world in Vienna, and the time she would spend there, from 1792 to 1795, would be so personally and professionally rewarding that she would always feel indebted to the Austrian ambassador Wilczek for having steered her in the right direction at a critical juncture of her life and career (I, 266).

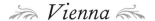 *Vienna*

WHEN VIGÉE LE BRUN arrived in Vienna, Austria had recently entered into war with revolutionary France. Maria Theresa, the powerful mother of Marie-Antoinette, had, among her other accomplishments, increased the reputation of Vienna as a center of the arts, and especially of music. After her death in 1780, her son and successor, Joseph II, impelled by the ideals of the Enlightenment, somewhat impetuously carried forward the reforms she had cautiously undertaken. When he died in 1790, he was succeeded by his brother Leopold II, who at first seemed receptive to the French revolutionary cause and hoped to avoid a war with revolutionary France. But after the unsuccessful attempt of the French royal family to flee from France and their arrest in Varennes, he gave in to the pressure of the Viennese as well as the émigrés eager to save Marie-Antoinette, daughter of their great empress, and therefore subscribed to the Declaration of Pillnitz of August 1791, which aimed at restoring Louis XVI as king of France, by force if necessary.

In March of 1792 Leopold II died rather suddenly as a result of illness and was succeeded by his son Francis II, as war between Austria and France was about to break out in April of that year. Francis II vigorously pursued a repressive policy aimed at quelling all subversive ideas or movements which might threaten the Austrian Empire.

As a staunch Royalist and official portraitist of Marie-Antoinette, Vigée Le Brun had of course been preceded by her renown on her arrival in Vienna. No wonder, therefore, that she was warmly welcomed in the Austrian capital. Armed with letters of recommendation, she was promptly admitted to the most exclusive Viennese salons, as well as to all important functions, and her life seemed to resume a pattern she had established in Paris before 1789. Since all the aristocrats in Vienna, whether Austrian, Russian, or Polish, spoke perfect French and cultivated the kind of wit and courtly elegance typical of prerevolutionary French aristocracy, Vigée Le Brun felt almost at home. Social life in Vienna was brilliant, and as an ardent music lover she eagerly attended fine concerts, especially appreciating full orchestra performances of some of Haydn's symphonies (I, 282). She was also invited to the great balls given by emperor Francis II and by the Russian ambassador, Count Rasomovski. There she observed for the first time such new dances as the waltz and the polonaise: "They danced the waltz with such frenzy that I could not imagine how all these people, spinning around at such rate, did not get giddy and fall down; but men and women are so accustomed to this violent exercise that they did not take a single break as long as the ball lasted. They also frequently danced the Polonaise, far less fatiguing, for it is nothing more than a procession during which twosomes promenade in stately fashion. It marvelously suits pretty women as it affords all the necessary time to admire their figures and faces" (I, 281).

In a desire to show that she was also sensitive to the living conditions of ordinary people, she made it a point to underscore in her autobiography that even the most menial workers and peasants were well dressed and had an air "of contentment and well-being," and that she never saw a single beggar, either in the city proper or in its surroundings

(I, 279). She also wholeheartedly approved of the fact that the richest Viennese families showed great benevolence in their philanthropic endeavors and gave generous portions of their immense incomes to the poor (I, 279).

Vigée Le Brun spent more than two years in Vienna and was as happy as one could possibly be "far from one's family and homeland" (I, 288). Once more, she was able to combine an active social life with a rigorous schedule as an artist, and with her customary energy she also thoroughly explored the Austrian capital, its grandiose palaces, and especially its art museums and galleries replete with works by the greatest masters, including such special favorites of hers as Rubens and Van Dyck.

Because of the great influx of émigrés, it was nearly impossible at first to find proper living accommodations in the city proper. Vigée Le Brun therefore rented a house in the suburbs and shared it with the Bistris, the Polish couple she had recently befriended in Milan, and the portrait she painted of the beautiful countess was the first of several she would execute in the Austrian capital. Indeed, there were so many lovely women in the Viennese salons that Vigée Le Brun found it difficult to single out some of them for portrayal. After the Bistris returned to Poland, she decided that it was more practical to meet her numerous professional and related social obligations by moving to the city proper. But she needed to alternate the excitement and stimulation of city life with the peaceful, refreshing, and slower rhythms of country life. With the advent of spring, she therefore also rented a small house in a little village called Huitzing, well situated within striking distance of the Austrian capital and in the vicinity of the Danube as well as the famed Schönbrunn Palace and Park. Here she was able to resume one of her favorite pastimes, which consisted, as she puts it in terms strikingly reminiscent of Rousseau, of taking long, solitary walks (I, 287).[1]

In this respect, as in so many others, Vigée Le Brun was a disciple of Rousseau, especially in his role as a lover of nature and as an introspective dreamer and wanderer, an influence she would not readily acknowledge for obvious political reasons. Indeed, she was so taken with the picturesque sites she came upon in her walks that she would frequently take along her pastels and, happily settling down on the banks of the Danube, endeavor to capture in studies and sketches the river, trees, and distant mountains.

Shortly after her arrival in Vienna, news from France became increasingly alarming. In the midst of a brilliant round of social activities and numerous portrait commissions she received constant reminders of the dire events unfolding in her homeland. Learning through current gazettes of the trials and executions of so many friends and acquaintances plunged her in a state of such depression that her friends conspired to withhold the latest news accounts from her.

In her autobiography Vigée Le Brun asserts that a letter from her brother Etienne, who had remained in Paris, informed her of the public beheading by the guillotine of Louis XVI on January 21, 1793,[2] and that of Marie-Antoinette, on October 16 of the same year:[3] "I learned of the horrible event from my brother, who wrote to me without adding any further detail. Heartbroken, he merely told me that Louis XVI and Marie-Antoinette had died on the scaffold!" (I, 285). It is probably for reasons of political prudence as much as in order to spare his sister's feelings that Etienne Vigée refrained from elaborating on this horrific piece of news. It is also likely, as well, that she had been apprised of the guillotining of Louis XVI and Marie-Antoinette through other channels emanating more directly from the Austrian court. Be that as it may, she must have experienced a sense of real horror at losing in such dreadful circumstances a woman she had always looked upon as a kindly friend and generous patroness. She was so deeply shocked by this news that she consistently refrained from making any further references or inquiries about the circumstances of what she viewed as an "awful assassination"

(I, 285). And indeed, she must have been filled with a profound sense of outrage to learn that the charming, kindly young woman who had so graciously posed for so many portraits and played such a key role in furthering her career as an artist had been brutally guillotined before a huge crowd raucously celebrating this bloody deed (fig. 11). She now fully realized that a return to France in the foreseeable future was out of the question.

Probably out of an instinct for personal survival, and in order to avoid giving into the kind of debilitating depression she was prone to in times of great stress and to be able to continue functioning as a self-sustaining artist with many portrait commissions on her hands, Vigée Le Brun made a conscious, deliberate effort to inure herself against the adverse effect that Marie-Antoinette's tragic death might have on her own physical and mental health. Her reaction, in this respect, which might strike one as selfish and even heartless, is understandable in light of her own precarious situation. More than ever she needed to be in full possession of her faculties so that she could pursue her singular career as an independent woman artist in a Europe torn by strife and revolution.

Some of the other émigrés women in the entourage of the Habsburg Court fared less well than Vigée Le Brun in coping with the dire political developments in France. This was notably the case of the Duchess Yolande de Polignac, one of the friendly acquaintances Vigée Le Brun had made as portraitist of Marie-Antoinette (see plate 10). She, too, had emigrated to Austria and happened to reside in Vigée Le Brun's immediate vicinity. The ravishingly beautiful Duchess de Polignac, propelled by her ambitious family, had become a member of the queen's exclusive group of female intimates. The queen especially enjoyed her company because she had no intellectual pretensions and was a delightful, undemanding companion. Yet even before the Revolution, all kinds of defamatory rumors had swirled around the close friendship between

FIG. 11. *Jacques-Louis David*, Sketch of Marie-Antoinette on the Way to the Guillotine. *Musée National du Louvre, Paris. (Réunion des Musées Nationaux/ Art Resource, NY)*

the queen and the duchess, especially one that clearly intimated that they were actually a lesbian couple.[4] In her memoir Vigée Le Brun undertakes a vigorous defense of the moral character of the duchess, asserting that she was the most innocent and guileless of women and a specially targeted victim of sheer, malicious calumny: "Everyone who knew her intimately can confirm how understandable it was that the queen had chosen her as her friend" (II, 299). Indeed, Vigée Le Brun endeavors to depict her as a rather passive, indolent person who aspired above all to privacy and who took no pleasure in the demanding duties as governess of the children of Louis XVI and Marie-Antoinette, a position she had reluctantly assumed in 1780 upon the insistence of the royal couple. Having taken refuge in Austria after the Revolution, the duchess was so profoundly affected by the news of the death of Louis XVI, and especially that of Marie-Antoinette, that she fell into a state of deep prostration from which she never recovered: "Her grief transformed her so completely that her charming features became unrecognizable and that one could predict her forthcoming end. She did indeed die shortly afterwards, leaving her family and friends who had not left her side inconsolable of her loss" (I, 284).

One of the most notable portraits Vigée Le Brun executed in Vienna is that of Countess Bucquoi (fig. 12), and it reflects a new style of pre-Romantic poetic portraiture she had developed since painting the portrait of Countess Potocka in Rome (see fig. 17). It consists in integrating the portrait of an attractive young woman seated in a pleasingly pensive mode with a dramatic landscape backdrop featuring such picturesque elements favored by the emerging Romantic sensibility as grottoes, trees, mountains, and waterfalls.

Countess Bucquoi is shown facing the onlooker, a slight smile playing on her lips. Her pleasingly regular and youthful features are framed by abundant and loose, curly hair freely falling to her shoulders partially covered by a turbanlike headdress. Her left hand gently supports her

FIG. 12. *Elisabeth Vigée Le Brun*, Portrait of Countess Bucquoi, *1793*. The *Minneapolis Institute of Arts, Minnesota*.

head, and her other hand is resting in her lap. The overall color scheme is quite intense, with a predominance of reds, yet softened by the landscape background consisting of trees, mountains, and a cascading waterfall.

Another notable portrait Vigée Le Brun executed in Vienna is that of Countess Von Schönfeld and her daughter (fig. 13). Here for the first time since going into exile she reverted to the theme of motherhood she had treated in portraits of herself and her daughter, Julie, in 1786 and 1789. The pose is particularly reminiscent of the 1786 self-portrait with Julie. The handsome young countess is seated, holding her small daughter in a tender, loving embrace. What mainly differentiates this appealing scene of motherhood from the two previous ones is the background. Here it is no longer a merely neutral, enclosed space, but opens up onto a Romantic landscape with trees, distant mountains, and a luminous sky.

This portraiture of mother love must have had an autobiographical component, for ever since having fled from France under dramatic circumstances with her young daughter in tow, Vigée Le Brun had gone out of her way to compensate for the absence of a fixed home and a normal family life by providing Julie with as pleasant surroundings as she could secure and with a host of tutors charged with giving the child as thorough an education as possible. Vigée Le Brun's exceptionally successful but precariously nomadic artistic career must have had an adverse impact on young Julie.

As an avid reader of Rousseau, Vigée Le Brun had to be keenly aware of the strong emphasis the author of *Emile* placed on the role of women as keepers of the hearth and home and on their main biological and social function, which is to bear and nurture the young, thereby assuring the survival of the species.[5] While she never seemed to have pondered consciously her own exceptional situation as an artist and self-supporting mother, for introversion and self-analysis were not her forte, she must have at times experienced a lingering sense of guilt at

FIG. 13. *Elisabeth Vigée Le Brun*, Portrait of Countess Von Schönfeld and Her Daughter, *1793. Collection of The University of Arizona Museum of Art, Tucson, Gift of Samuel H. Kress Foundation.*

failing to live up to Rousseau's ideal of womanly domesticity and motherhood.

Meanwhile in France, her husband's repeated efforts on her behalf came to naught. In spite of his marital infidelities and profligate habits, Jean-Baptiste Le Brun was in his own way a loyal and supportive husband who early on had recognized his wife's exceptional talent and had actively furthered her career. Now that she was an *émigrée* he exerted himself at his own risk in order to exonerate her name. On March 28, 1793, he published a pamphlet titled *Historical Summary of the Life of Citizen Le Brun, Painter (Précis historique de la vie de la citoyenne Le Brun, peintre)*, in which he strenuously undertook the defense of her artistic and moral integrity and stressed the fact that the so-called fortune she had allegedly made under the Old Regime now merely consisted of two heavily mortgaged houses. The pamphlet obviously failed to convince the revolutionary authorities, for when he followed it up on October 6 of the same year with a petition to have his wife considered not as a political émigré but as a painter who had left France for Italy in order to perfect her artistic knowledge, it also met with rejection. In November of the same year Le Brun himself was briefly incarcerated, and shortly thereafter Etienne Vigée, the artist's brother, was imprisoned until July of 1794. As the Terror raged, Le Brun found himself forced to divorce his wife on the grounds of desertion in order to avoid further personal persecution and property confiscation. On June 3, 1794, a decree of divorce was issued.

Having given up the idea of returning to France, Vigée Le Brun established a routine reminiscent of her life in prerevolutionary Paris. After a full day's work at the easel she would spend the evenings enjoying Vienna's brilliant society, balls, concerts, and plays, including private amateur theatricals, of which she had always been especially fond. She had no thought of leaving Austria, but some of the friends she had made among the nobles and notable political figures in Austria, notably the Russian ambassador and several of his compatriots, insistently assured her that an immensely wealthy aristocratic clientele awaited her in Saint Petersburg and that Empress Catherine II herself would be very pleased to have her at her court.

Also among those urging her to go to Russia was the amiable and eminently cultured Prince de Ligne. Born a Habsburg subject, he had been an intimate of Maria Theresa and Joseph II, and could also boast of enjoying a personal relationship with Catherine II (II, 294). Vigée Le Brun had originally met him during her 1781 tour of Holland and Flanders and had enjoyed his hospitality at his superb estate of Beloeil near Brussels.[6] He, in turn, became a frequent guest at her soirées after his arrival in Paris a few years before the Revolution, for they obviously liked each other's company. The Revolution ruined him financially, and, with his Belgian estates confiscated, he emigrated to Vienna where he had to live in rather straitened circumstances. Although not a born Frenchman, he was an ardent Francophile and had so thoroughly mastered the French language and culture that, in the words of his fellow cosmopolitan Germaine de Staël, "he was perhaps the only foreigner who in this respect had become a model rather than an imitator" (II, 293). As a matter of fact, numerous volumes of his *Military, Literary, and Sentimental Miscellany (Mélanges militaires, littéraires, et sentimentaux)* came off the presses of Dresden and Vienna fairly regularly between 1795 and 1811 and remained largely unnoticed by the public until Germaine de Staël collected and published a selection, titled *Letters and Reflections of the Prince de Ligne (Lettres et réflexions du prince de Ligne)*, in 1809. It is doubtless this edition that Vigée Le Brun read and warmly praised in her own memoir (II, 294).

Ever since she had gone into exile with almost no money, Vigée Le Brun was intent on rebuilding her fortune so that when political circumstances would eventually enable her to return to her homeland she would be financially secure and independent. To be sure, she did not lack for lucrative commissions in Vienna, but the huge properties and riches of Russian aristocrats and, of course, of Catherine II herself, were truly mind-boggling. She therefore reasoned, with characteristic pragmatism, that this was an opportunity not to be missed. Besides, always eager to embark on a new travel venture, she increasingly warmed to the prospect of discovering firsthand a vast, mysterious land so little known by most Westerners. She therefore began making all the necessary arrangements for her big move to the imperial court of Saint Petersburg. The always attentive Prince de Ligne advised her to avoid making the trip during the harsh Russian winter months.

Thus it was that on April 19, 1795, Vigée Le Brun left the Austrian capital, where she had spent two and a half years that had been generally rewarding, both personally and professionally. While she was eager to reach her destination, she stopped off in Prague, Dresden, and Berlin, primarily to visit famed natural sites, cathedrals, and art collections. She reached Prague on April 23, where she spent only one hectic day, barely managing to take notice of the picturesque features of the city and its artistic treasures (I, 293). Dresden retained her somewhat longer, for she was intent on exploring its famous Art Gallery, which she deemed "the most beautiful in Europe" and to which she paid repeated visits during her stay in the city (I, 294). From Dresden she proceeded to Berlin, where she stayed for only five days, intending to return there on her eventual way back from Russia (I, 297). But even this brief stay in the capital of Prussia enabled her to visit its principal sites, art collections, and royal palaces. She was especially aware, both in Berlin and especially in Potsdam, of the hovering presence of Frederick the Great, who had died in 1786: "I sat down on the bench where sat the great the soldier-king. From there he enjoyed the most beautiful view of the world" (I, 298). The comment may strike one as disappointingly banal and superficial for one who had painted the portraits of some of the most notable rulers of Europe, and in the process had been on fairly intimate terms with her sitters and must have gained some rare insights into their mentality as well as into the inner workings of absolute power. But Vigée Le Brun was not given to elaborate on her innermost thoughts and emotions in *Souvenirs,* for unlike Rousseau she did not think that the autobiographer should be confessional and owed it to the reader to tell all. As a staunch monarchist, however, she was bound to admire a powerful, even ruthless, autocrat like Frederick the Great who, unlike the hapless Louis XVI, knew how to wield and hold onto absolute power and at the same time also cultivate his image as an "enlightened despot," mainly through his highly publicized friendship with Voltaire, d'Alembert, and other philosophes.[7]

After these detours through Prague, Dresden, and Berlin, Vigée Le Brun embarked on the final stages of her journey to Saint Petersburg. The coach first passed through prosperous-looking small towns and fertile fields, but progress was slow and the ride uncomfortably bumpy, owing to poor roads. In Riga, she took a much needed rest of a few days while passports for Saint Petersburg were being issued. Thereafter, the roads grew even worse, so that the travelers were constantly shaken and jolted, and the inns along the way were so awful as to preclude any possibility of stopping off at any of them, as was then customary on such long journeys.[8] But always the Royalist, Vigée Le Brun points out in *Souvenirs* that Czar Alexander I had the road completely rebuilt, so that travelers no longer faced her kind of harrowing experience (I, 303).

Exhausted but also exhilarated, Vigée Le Brun reached at last the imperial capital on July 25, 1795, entering it by way of the Peterhoff road, which was lined on either side with handsome country houses and lovely gardens in the English style made possible by the marshy soil and adorned with small bridges, streams, and canals.

CHAPTER TEN

❧ *The Russian Experience* ❧

VIGÉE LE BRUN had reached her fortieth birthday when she arrived in Saint Petersburg in the summer of 1795, but she had lost none of her enthusiasm, energy, and eagerness to test herself in the face of challenging new adventures and experiences.

The city itself was a creation by the sheer willpower of Peter the Great at the dawn of the eighteenth century in order to provide for Russia an outlet to the sea and a port of trade through the Baltic. More importantly, he wanted it to be not only the new Russian capital and a modern metropolis, but also "a window looking on Europe."[1] The building of a great metropolis on the marshy soil in the delta of the Neva River was carried out at huge human and material cost. Notable Italian and French architects planned the city for Peter and his successors, and the result of their work was a uniquely homogeneous, spacious, classical urban conglomerate.

Vigée Le Brun's first impression, after a few days' rest in order to recover from her fatigue, was that of a magnificent capital, with its splendid palaces, cathedrals, monuments, and wide streets; majestic edifices gracing the banks of the Neva River, which traverses the city carrying a colorful array of numerous ships and boats of all kinds; and intricate system of canals, waterways, and bridges. She was intrigued and visually stimulated by the rich and exotic mixture of styles the city presented: Western and Asian, classical and Baroque, cosmopolitan and provincial. She was told that there was no more stunning a sight than the shimmering Neva River in the moonlight, but she had to postpone this experience because her arrival in July coincided with the famous "white nights" of Saint Petersburg, when there is not a single hour of darkness. In *Souvenirs* she recalls having supped "at eleven o'clock in broad daylight" (I, 303).

In the decades immediately preceding Vigée Le Brun's stay in Russia, Saint Petersburg had reached the acme of its prestige and influence and, according to its many Western visitors, could rival Vienna and even Paris as a cosmopolitan and cultural mecca. Ever since rising from obscurity as a minor German princess in order to become the wife of the future Czar Peter III, and beginning her rule by a coup d'état on July 6, 1762, after her erratic, abusive, and unpopular husband's mysterious demise, Catherine II had promoted special ties with the French, and especially with the philosophes (fig. 14). She had steeped herself in the writings of Montesquieu, and her initial aim was probably to become known as an "enlightened" ruler, as her 1767 *Nakaz*, a new code of laws modeled after *The Spirit of the Laws,* testifies. It was published with great fanfare but never enacted. She also cultivated a highly publicized epistolary friendship with Voltaire and d'Alembert, and took a personal interest in the beleaguered Diderot and his *Encyclopédie,* who, in turn, as an art critic felt sufficiently knowledgeable in this field to advise her on some major purchases for her collection.[2] He also finally accepted in 1773 her repeated invitations to be her personal guest in Saint Petersburg, for like Voltaire he had succumbed to the temptation that he could win her over to truly "enlightened" views of government.[3]

However, by the time Vigée Le Brun came to Russia in 1795,

FIG. 14. *Alexander Roslin*, Portrait of Catherine II, *1776. State Hermitage Museum, St. Petersburg.*

Catherine's enthusiasm for the French in general and the philosophes in particular had considerably cooled, primarily because of the French Revolution, which as an absolute autocrat she understandably viewed as an unmitigated disaster.[4]

As Vigée Le Brun was diligently exploring the artistic and cultural riches of the imperial capital, she was even more intent on establishing contact with the leading members of the Russian nobility and especially on meeting with the great Empress herself. But the thought of being presented to this powerful woman filled her with anxious anticipation as well as the dread of making some disastrous faux pas. When she was promptly informed that she had indeed been summoned to appear before Catherine, she realized, to her horror, that she did not have a formal court outfit for the occasion. Wearing instead a simple, unadorned muslin dress, she failed to meet another court etiquette by forgetting, in her excitement and embarrassment, to kiss Catherine's hand (I, 305–6). But she was promptly reassured by soothing and flattering words of welcome: "I am delighted, Madam, to receive you here; your reputation has preceded you. I greatly love the arts, and especially painting. I am not a connoisseur, but a mere amateur" (I, 306). The Empress furthermore seemed to take no notice of Vigée Le Brun's inappropriate attire and graciously expressed the hope that she might like Russia well enough to make her stay there a long one.

Catherine the Great, who in 1795 was in her mid-sixties, struck Vigée Le Brun as an unexpectedly small woman, at least physically: "I was at first extremely surprised to find her so short in stature; I had imagined her as prodigiously tall as her reputation. She was very stout, but still had a handsome face, which her white hair framed beautifully. Genius seemed to hover on her high forehead. Her eyes were gentle yet penetrating, her nose was quite Greek, her complexion was lively, and her features were very animated" (I, 306).

Shortly after this memorable audience, Vigée Le Brun learned that the Empress had given orders that she be given an apartment in the Imperial summer palace at Tsarskoe Selo, a few miles from Saint Petersburg, for she wanted to have her guest near her and be able to see her paint (I, 307). Less overwhelming than the huge Winter Palace, the summer residence of Tsarskoe Selo, despite its magnificence and luxurious profusion of monuments and ornaments, offered a relatively restful setting thanks primarily to its great park originally designed in the orderly and symmetrical French classical style, but subsequently modified in accordance with the new English predilection for natural-ness and informality. But while greatly flattered by Catherine's gracious invitation, Vigée Le Brun was intent on maintaining her independence: "I have always had the greatest need to enjoy my freedom, and in order to live according to my own way of life, I have always infinitely preferred living in my own home" (I, 307).

She was therefore hardly disappointed when she learned that no apartment in the palace could be made available for her, for one reason or another, in spite of the order of the empress. The hardly veiled hostil-ity of some of the Russian courtiers toward a French émigré may also have played a part in this.

Of course, Vigée Le Brun could not be unaware of Catherine's scandalous reputation as a woman with enormous sexual appetites, but she preferred to refer to them as the kind of weakness one also finds in kings, citing as examples Francis I and Louis XIV, whose personal failing in this respect, in her opinion, in no way "had an impact on the happiness of their subject" (II, 19). Her highly promising relationship with the empress of all Russias failed to fulfill its initial promise. It so happened that the empress was highly displeased with Vigée Le Brun's portrait of her two granddaughters, the Grand Duchesses Alexandra and Elena Pavlovna, then about thirteen and fourteen years old (fig. 15).

Vigée Le Brun had been delighted and inspired by these two pretty, young women: "Their faces were celestial, though with quite different

FIG. 15. *Elisabeth Vigée Le Brun*, Portrait of Grand Duchess Alexandra Pavlovna and Elena Pavlovna, Daughters of Paul I and Granddaughters of Catherine II, *1796. State Hermitage Museum, St. Petersburg.*

expressions. . . . The elder daughter, Alexandra, had a Grecian beauty
. . . but the face of the younger, Helen, had infinitely more refinement.
I had them posed together, holding and looking at a portrait of the
Empress; their costume was slightly Greek, very simple and modest"
(I, 324). She was therefore shocked to learn that Catherine was "scandal-
ized" by the painting, and especially by the unadorned, sleeveless dresses
worn by the grand duchesses. This bad piece of news had been conveyed
to Vigée Le Brun by Catherine's current favorite, the young Platon
Zubov, who had become her lover in 1789 and who exercised great
influence on public affairs since the death in 1791 of his predecessor
in the affections of the empress, the powerful Grigori Aleksandrovich
Potemkin. In a panic Vigée Le Brun hastened to change the costume
of her subjects, covering their exposed lovely arms with bulky long
sleeves, and learned from Catherine herself that she had decided to
like the revised portrait. But it was too late. Vigée Le Brun felt that she
had "spoiled" her composition with these changes. This controversial
portrait nevertheless contributed to the vogue of the so-called Greek
style in Russian portraiture.

That Zubov was an incompetent and insecure intriguer who exercised his corrupt influence behind the scenes and shamelessly took
advantage of the aging tsarina became clear to Vigée Le Brun only later,
when it was pointed out to her that he resented and was envious of her
popularity at the Russian court, for the nobility flocked to her studio
and she was plied with constant invitations to attend dinners and balls.
In spite of Zubov's hostility, courtly patronage continued unabated and
numerous commissions for portraits of fabulously wealthy Russians provided Vigée Le Brun with handsome earnings. Throughout her stay in
Russia she kept up a very profitable productivity, turning out numerous
portraits which clearly show that she had lost none of her remarkable
skills. However, in *Souvenirs* she maintains that a good part of her Russian earnings was lost through an act of outright theft in her house while

she was at the theater, and she states that this financial loss was later compounded by a banker's dishonesty and bankruptcy (I, 319–20).

As an experienced court painter, Vigée Le Brun had gained considerable practice in dealing with intrigue, and just as she had charmed Marie-Antoinette she seems to have gotten into Catherine's good graces, in spite of the latter's wariness of all things French. Indeed, Vigée Le Brun was scheduled to paint the empress but was thwarted in this important project when she learned that Catherine had suddenly died of a stroke on November 17, 1796. The two women had met only a few days before and the tsarina had playfully remarked: "They absolutely want you to do my portrait. I am quite old, but since they all insist on it, I shall grant you the first session a week from today" (II, 23). As a result of these unforeseen circumstances, Vigée Le Brun managed to draw only an unfinished pastel sketch of Catherine.

In *Souvenirs* Vigée Le Brun presents a glowing account of Catherine the Great's accomplishments, especially as a benefactress of the Russian people, a great and enlightened leader who strongly supported and encouraged the arts, and a proponent of the latest medical advances, including vaccination against smallpox. She pays tribute to the tsarina's creation of the Hermitage, to her mastery of the French language in all its elegance and clarity. Her admiration for Catherine seems genuine, and she states that she viewed with reverence in a Saint Petersburg library the original manuscript of her famous "Instruction," written in French and entirely in her own hand (II, 20). This is an accurate description, for the lengthy "Instruction," which expounds Catherine's vision of great reforms and of how Russia should be governed, was indeed written entirely by her.[5]

Catherine doubtless wanted to present her own credentials as an enlightened monarch as well as to emulate Frederick II of Prussia, who had written the celebrated *Anti-Machiavel* in 1739, an idealistic refutation of Machiavelli which argued that armed aggression is immoral and that honesty the best policy for a ruler, maxims that Frederick blatantly contradicted in his own ruthless leadership and bold military tactics after his accession to the throne in 1740.[6]

Catherine's famous "Instruction," although written in her own hand, was by no means original in its conception. As an avid reader and admirer of Montesquieu, she drew largely from his *Spirit of the Laws* (1748) as well as from a recently published work by the Italian jurist Cesare Beccaria, *On Crimes and Punishments* (1763). Having seized the throne in June 1762, shortly after the murder of her feckless and unpopular husband, Peter III, she wanted to demonstrate that Russia was not an Asiatic despotic state ruled by fear, but rather a modern European monarchy ruled by reason.

Quite understandably, Vigée Le Brun was especially impressed by Catherine's great contribution to the arts and by her powerful patronage of painting, sculpture, and architecture. The empress was an avid, indeed compulsive, art collector and was doubtless motivated by politics as well as a truly passionate love of art. She laid the foundations of the extraordinarily rich collection still displayed today in the Hermitage Museum of the Winter Palace in Saint Petersburg.[7] She bought such famed foreign collections as the one that had belonged to Sir Robert Walpole and another that was part of the estate of the French Baron Thiers, negotiated for her by Diderot in 1772. Vigée Le Brun is especially impressed with Catherine's creation of the Hermitage, which by the end of the eighteenth century "had become one of Europe's most important museums."[8]

Vigée Le Brun also takes obvious pleasure in stressing the fact that Catherine's accomplishments as a great monarch were on a par with those of the most notable male rulers and mischievously cites the Prince de Ligne's quip that one could rightly call the autocrat of all Russias "Catherine le Grand," rather than "Catherine la Grande" (II, 19), a sly and discreet way of alluding to the fact that a woman had demonstrated that she could wield the scepter over a huge empire as well as a man could. She probably also derived satisfaction subconsciously from the parallel with her own situation as a female painter who had learned to handle the paintbrush as masterfully as her most gifted and successful male counterparts. What also struck Vigée Le Brun was that this absolute monarch was actually "the simplest and least demanding woman" in her private life. She would, for instance, get up at five in the morning and make her own coffee (II, 20).

Vigée Le Brun was not only warmly received and sought after by the noblest and wealthiest members of the most select society of Saint Petersburg, she also became a center of attraction of the French émigrés who, like her, had ended up in Russia. Elegant and beautiful Russian young women of the highest nobility, in particular, wanted to be painted by her. In spite of the Revolution, Russian aristocrats still craved for all things French and were fascinated and intrigued by Vigée Le Brun's celebrity as a fashionable portraitist, as a bold trendsetter, as one who had innovated a new style of portraiture by dressing her subjects in fluid, light, loosely draped gowns, and who as a hostess in Paris had been able to gather in her salon some of the most notable personalities of the French nobility and artistic elite and who had even caused something of a scandal with her famous Greek supper in her Rue de Cléry residence. No wonder, therefore, that Vigée Le Brun painted some of her most seductive portraits of women while in Russia.

The style she favored for these portraits aimed at seizing the subject in an intimate, unselfconscious and introspective moment of reflection. One such portrait is that of Princess Dolgorouky, painted in 1797 (private collection).[9] Catherine Feodorovna Dolgorouky hosted one of the most fashionable salons in Saint Petersburg, and before long Vigée Le Brun and her daughter, Julie, were among her guests in her country estate in Alexandrowski. There the princess lavishly entertained her guests with dinners, concerts, amateur performances in her own intimate theater, where Vigée Le Brun had the opportunity of staging "tableaux vivants," or scenes inspired by the bible or mythology, with the most handsome men and women adorned in historical costume. There were also leisurely boat rides in which the rowers sang in chorus Russian songs, which struck her as "melancholy and melodious" (II, 312).

The princess greatly admired Vigée Le Brun's portrait of Lady Hamilton as a sibyl and insisted that her own portrait be painted in the same style. The pose and costume are indeed closely derived from the 1791 portrait of Lady Hamilton, which was one of Vigée Le Brun's personal favorites and which she carried with her throughout her European peregrinations. The princess had therefore had the opportunity to see it in Vigée Le Brun's studio.

It is a portrait that aims at raising mere portraiture, officially relegated to genre painting, to the more exalted level of historical composition. The princess is shown seated, leaning on her right elbow, which is lightly resting on a round marble table bearing open books, among which is Locke's famous 1693 treatise on education, as well as some musical scores, reflecting the subject's strong cultural interests and activities. A turbanlike headdress enhances her lovely, somewhat exotic features, and a simple gown discreetly molds her youthful, slim figure. Her pose suggests that she has briefly suspended her reading of Locke for a few moments of thoughtful reflection. The overall effect of the composition is less theatrical and melodramatic, more natural and subdued than the portrait of Emma Hamilton as a sibyl. Le Brun had been greatly taken by the beauty, amiability, hospitality, and generosity of Princess Dolgorouky (II, 312), who handsomely rewarded her for her work with a carriage and diamond necklace.

Yet another variation on her style of female portraiture she used to good effect while in Russia is a genteel combination of neoclassicism and romanticism. Her subject would be dressed in a free-flowing gown "à l'antique," while the background would be a landscape of trees, mountains, and vast expanse of sky. One such striking portrait is that of Julie Le Brun as Flora, goddess of flowers, executed in 1799 in Saint Petersburg (private collection).

By the time Vigée Le Brun had arrived in Saint Petersburg, the powerful Grigori Aleksandrovich Potemkin, who had been Catherine's favorite from 1774 until his death in 1791 and who had played a key political role in her reign, had long been gone from the scene. Yet his presence was still strongly felt, and he was still a frequent subject of conversation and gossip. Thus Vigée Le Brun makes mention of the famous allegation that he built sham villages along her Crimean route of 1787 by referring to "these palaces, these villages, built like by a magic wand" (I, 316). When the youthful but inept Zubov replaced him in the affections of the aging Catherine in 1789, the same Zubov who had initially intrigued against Vigée Le Brun, he was unable to survive Potemkin's disgrace.

The closest personal friends Vigée Le Brun made in Russia were Princesses Dolgorouky and especially Natalya Kurakina, the confidante to whom she would address the first part of her *Souvenirs*, couched as informal, intimate letters. Natalya Kurakina belonged to one of the most powerful and richest families of Russian landowners on whose large estates an army of serfs labored in various capacities.[10]

Catherine's sudden death on November 17, 1796, plunged the Russian nation in a state of grief and dread. The populace gave vent to its grief in large but generally quiet and subdued gatherings in front of the Saint Petersburg Palace. Her body was exposed for six weeks in a stateroom of the palace, lit up day and night and lavishly decorated. She was laid out on a bed of state, surrounded by shields bearing the arms of all the towns in the empire: "Her face was uncovered, her beautiful hand resting on the bed" (II, 25).

Catherine's reign had lasted thirty-four years and had been deeply marked by her strong personality. She had been a woman of a positive temperament, unlike the moody Potemkin.[11] She had been a great ruler, imbued with a profound sense of the crucial role destiny had entrusted her to play as tsarina of all Russias. In this respect Vigée Le Brun's testimony of Catherine as a woman with an enormous breadth of intellectual and cultural curiosity, an awesome capacity for hard work, simple personal tastes, and charm and dignity in her manners and behavior is fully borne out by historians.[12]

With Catherine's death there was a general feeling that a great epoch had come to a close, and anxious attention focused on the character of her son and successor, the Grand Duke Paul. Catherine herself had strongly disliked him and attempted on several occasions to change the succession to his disadvantage. No wonder, therefore, that the new tsar Paul did not share in the national sense of sorrow and loss upon the death of Catherine. He ascended to the throne on December 12, 1796, as Paul I, emperor of all Russias.

In her memoir Vigée Le Brun describes him as physically ugly, with a snub nose and large mouth which favored caricatures. He was energetic and clever but vindictive, paranoid, and prone to whims bordering on insanity. His character was basically unstable, and acts of generosity would immediately be followed by outbursts of rage and paranoia (II, 27).

Under Paul the regime became very repressive: "The least infraction to Paul's orders was punished with exile to Siberia, or at the very least to imprisonment" (II, 28). The result was that people lived in a state of perpetual anxiety and even feared to invite friends to their houses. Everyone's words and actions were watched, and shutters would be closed to attempt to protect the privacy of the meetings of friends. Everyone abstained from making comments on the new tsar for fear of dreadful reprisals.

Paul treated Vigée Le Brun with great courtesy, for he had a personal partiality for the French, and she was even commissioned to paint the portrait of his wife, Empress Maria, a tall, handsome woman whose appearance contrasted sharply with that of her homely husband. She was also kindly, and during the sittings Paul himself appeared once and offered a cup of coffee to the artist (II, 39). Yet Vigée Le Brun experienced under Paul's reign a sense of terror reminiscent of what she had gone through in revolutionary Paris. She could not explain this sense of dread in rational terms, except that it was part of a climate of fear and uncertainty that pervaded Russian society after the death of Catherine and the end of her generally benevolent reign (II, 30).

Professionally, however, Vigée Le Brun derived much satisfaction from continued recognition and appreciation of her work. On June 16, 1800, she was made an honorary free associate of the Imperial Academy of Arts of Saint Petersburg. During the reception ceremony Count Alexander Stroganov, president of the Academy, made a laudatory speech and handed her the official diploma, at which time there was such thunderous applause from the spectators that it brought tears to her eyes and made it one of the most memorable occasions she experienced in Russia (II, 48).

At long last the campaign in France on behalf of Vigée Le Brun by her husband as well as friends and admirers to rehabilitate the exiled artist began to pay off. After the end of the Terror, marked by the coup d'état of 9 Thermidor (July 27, 1794) and culminating in the arrest and execution of Robespierre, a new regime, the Directory, was voted into power in 1795. The period of the Thermidorian Convention and the Directory (July 7, 1794–November 10, 1799) signaled the actual end of the Revolution. As a result, there was a softening of attitudes toward émigrés, and the cause of Vigée Le Brun benefited from this dramatic change in political climate.

In 1796 Marie-Victoire Lemoine (1750–1820), a portraitist and genre painter, exhibited in the Salon a composition titled *Interior of the*

Atelier of a Woman Painter (New York, The Metropolitan Museum of Art). It is a self-portrait showing her seated on a low stool, at work at the feet of the standing and attractive figure of Vigée Le Brun, dressed in a simple white gown, holding a palette in her left hand and gazing at a large, unfinished composition on an easel. Lemoine had actually never studied with Vigée Le Brun, who had hardly enjoyed her brief experience as an art instructor. The composition, therefore, was doubtless meant to be a tribute, a symbolic homage to the celebrated exiled portraitist.[13] The Paris Salon of 1798 exhibited two recent paintings by Vigée Le Brun, and on July 26, 1799, a delegation of artists presented a petition on her behalf bearing 255 signatures.[14]

During her stay in Russia Vigée Le Brun's relationship with her twenty-year-old daughter, Julie, became increasingly strained. Under trying circumstances she had always done her best as a mother, had never separated from her during her peripatetic years, had provided her with excellent teachers, and doted on her more than ever, for she looked upon her as a source of joy and comfort as she envisioned her own approaching waning years (II, 50).

Julie was an attractive, accomplished young woman, with large, expressive blue eyes, a slightly upturned nose, full lips, and a pleasingly slim figure. She spoke several languages, including Italian, German, and Russian. She played the piano and the guitar, had a pleasing singing voice, knew how to draw and paint, and enjoyed writing romance stories. Her unusually cosmopolitan background and contacts with members of the highest European society had endowed her with a polish and sophistication beyond her age.

Vigée Le Brun had enriched her own artistic inspiration by depicting Julie in all the stages of her young life, from the time she was an infant cuddling in her mother's loving embrace until she reached adolescence, when her mother painted her in the seductive guise of Flora, goddess of flowers and fertility, holding a basket of flowers on her head and dressed in a sleeveless, diaphanous white gown (1799, private collection).[15]

But as Julie grew into young womanhood she increasingly rebelled against her powerful and possessive mother. A major crisis occurred when, in the fall of 1800, Julie peremptorily announced that she had fallen in love with and would marry Gaétan Bernard Nigris, secretary to Count Grigorii Czernicheff, the director of the Imperial Theaters of Saint Petersburg. The count's wife had befriended Julie, and while Vigée Le Brun was busy at her easel her daughter was being invited to various social entertainments and diversions by the countess, such as sleigh rides. This is how she met Nigris, a rather good-looking thirty-year-old man whose pensive expression and slight pallor gave him a romantic aura that made him irresistibly attractive to Julie. Aside from his minor position, the notion of giving her beloved daughter and only child to a man "without talent, without fortune, without name" (II, 50) was unbearable. She made discreet inquiries about him and received conflicting reports about his character, and she tried in vain to make Julie understand that this marriage would be unlikely to make her happy.

Under all this stress Julie fell ill, and her mother surrendered. But under existing laws no marriage could take place without the consent of the father. Vigée Le Brun therefore wrote to her estranged husband in Paris in order to obtain his legal approval. The separated spouses had remained in epistolary contact, and both had hoped that their daughter would agree to marry Pierre-Narcisse Guérin (1774–1833), a brilliant young artist who had won the Grand Prix de Rome in 1797 and obtained great success in exhibiting in the 1799 Salon a neoclassical composition titled *The Return of Belisarius to His Family*, which was deemed worthy of Jacques-Louis David's 1781 famous *Belisarius*, depicting the great Roman general reduced to begging (II, 52). Generally looked upon as David's spiritual heir, Guérin would have been a fine match for the daughter of a famous portraitist and a renowned art dealer. And indeed, Guérin's artistic career would turn out to be a distinguished one not only as one of the best neoclassical painters of his generation, but also as the teacher of such masters as Théodore Géricault and Eugène Delacroix.[16]

The Le Bruns had to give up this fond dream, and Julie was allowed to marry Nigris. Vigée Le Brun even gave Julie a lavish dowry and trousseau, as well as jewelry, all derived from the handsome fees she had earned as a successful portraitist in Saint Petersburg (II, 53). She furthermore hastened to her daughter's bedside when shortly after the marriage she learned that Julie had contracted smallpox, an acute, highly contagious and frequently disfiguring disease. Fortunately, Julie recovered fully and bore no physical scars of her illness (II, 54). But the relationship between mother and daughter would never be the same after the marriage: "As for me, the whole charm of my life seemed to be irretrievably destroyed. I no longer felt the same joy in loving my daughter, although God knows how much I still cherished her, in spite of all her wrongdoing. Only mothers will fully understand me" (II, 53). Furthermore, Vigée Le Brun's negative evaluation of the character and future prospects of Nigris turned out to be basically accurate, and the marriage ended in failure. The couple would eventually separate after their return to Paris in 1804, and in 1808 Nigris went back alone to Saint Petersburg.

The events leading up to Julie's wedding and her illness left Vigée Le Brun in a state of physical exhaustion and mental depression. A change in scenery was deemed desirable. On October 15, 1800, Vigée Le Brun therefore left Saint Petersburg and set out for Moscow, which she had not yet visited and where she would remain until the following spring.

The journey was nightmarish, for the unpaved roads were atrocious, especially at this time of the year when the mud had not yet solidified into ice. The carriage swayed and rolled fearfully as though a ship on a stormy sea, and a thick fog hung over everything. Desperate for a brief rest and some food, she stopped at an inn in Novgorod, which turned out to be unbearably lugubrious and foul-smelling. When she was told that the source of the stench was the corpse of a man in the room adjoining hers, she promptly ordered horses harnessed to her carriage and resumed her trying journey, with only some bread to sustain her (II, 57).

At long last she reached Moscow and almost forgot her fatigue at the sight of the exotic grandeur of the spectacle it offered, its striking mixture of magnificence and rusticity, which she found unlike any other great city she had seen, including the more Europeanized Saint Petersburg. Indeed, she thought herself transported to Persia: "I seemed to be entering Isfahan, of which I had seen drawings, so starkly does Moscow differ from everything else in Europe. I will therefore not attempt to describe the effect produced by those thousands of gilded domes surmounted by huge gold crosses, those broad streets, those superb palaces. . . . To get an idea of Moscow, one must see it" (II, 57).

As soon as she settled down, she explored the city with her customary energy and curiosity as frequently as the rigors of the Russian winter allowed, its palaces, public monuments, churches, and especially the Kremlin, the historic core of Moscow with its fortress and its old palace of the czars. She noted that the city counted nearly a half a million inhabitants and that it had a thriving commerce, as evidenced by its numerous shops and colorful open markets. She marveled at the intermingling of palaces, churches, and convents with picturesque villages within the sprawling city, noting that this mixture of urban magnificence and rural simplicity was something she had never seen before in her extensive travels. Moscow cemeteries also fascinated her, especially the fact that huge crowds filled them on religious occasions, giving vent to their emotions in loud lamentations, and she took note of the fact that steam baths were as popular in Moscow as in Saint Petersburg, a practice she attributed to the fact that Russians were not prey to chest diseases or rheumatism (II, 60).

On the whole, however, Vigée Le Brun did not really enjoy her stay in Moscow, in spite of the fact that she was warmly welcomed by its noblest and most fabulously wealthy families. The temperature was consistently twenty degrees below freezing. She was dogged by a persistent housing problem, for the lodgings put at her disposal were either intolerably noisy or unbearably frigid. In the first mansion to which she was invited, her need for rest and tranquillity was constantly frustrated by a group of musicians who daily practiced in the grand salon (II, 58). She therefore decided to move and accepted the offer of hospitality graciously extended to her by Countess Catherine Strogonova, whose friendship and that of her husband went back to Vienna, to settle down in a small house that had long been unoccupied. But the house turned out to be so icy that in order to remedy this situation she had all the stoves heated to a maximum, with the result that on one night she was awakened by an asphyxiating smoke, and barely escaped with her life (II, 62).

A wonderfully revealing self-portrait of Vigée Le Brun, dated 1800 (plate 14) shows the forty-five-year-old artist at work in front of a canvas with the sketched outlines of a portrait of the Empress Maria Fedorovna, wife of Paul I. Her left hand holds a palette, and her right hand, armed with a brush, is gracefully suspended in mid-action as she faces the onlooker with a look of quiet and subdued self-confidence, a half-smile playing on her lips, and her finely chiseled features indicating subtle but unmistakable signs of aging and the effects of the wear and tear of her struggles and itinerant existence. She is demurely dressed in a dark, long-sleeved gown with a very modest décolleté, adorned with a gauze scarf wrapped around her waist and shoulders and discreetly veiling her slightly sagging neckline. A white turbanlike headdress covers her still curly but graying hair.

This is undoubtedly Vigée Le Brun's most intimate, restrained, sober, and profoundly spiritual self-portrait. It lacks the bravado and narcissism of her previous self-portraits of 1781 and 1790, where she had so proudly proclaimed both her youthful beauty and artistic pre-eminence. But it is relentlessly truthful in the representation of a middle-aged woman facing her declining physical beauty while also affirming her essential selfhood, dignity, and continued creativity as an artist. It is also a powerful affirmation of a woman's capacity for survival in the face of overwhelming odds against her as an artist.

During her five-month stay in Moscow Vigée Le Brun was eagerly sought after by the most aristocratic and wealthiest members of the city's society. She dined with the hugely rich Prince Alexander Kurakin, who would become Russian ambassador in France under Napoleon. She had already met him in Saint Petersburg, and it was rumored about him that he had in his sumptuous palace a real seraglio in the oriental style (II, 65). Yet she found him to be an affable, unpretentious man and had painted a fine portrait of him in 1797 (fig. 16). She had furthermore become very friendly with his sister-in-law, Princess Natalya Kurakina, to whom she would address the first part of her *Souvenirs,* couched as twelve lengthy letters written in the elegantly informal and intimate con-versational manner made popular by Madame de Sévigné's enormously influential epistolary work, so widely imitated by eighteenth-century women writers.[17] Princess Kurakina had indeed urged her painter-friend to write her memoirs, and it was at her insistence that Vigée Le Brun had finally overcome her scruples and hesitations and decided to tell the story of her long and eventful life, as she acknowledges at the very outset of her *Souvenirs* (I, 23).

Vigée Le Brun also socialized with the powerful but aging Prince Dimitri Galitzin, whose vast art collection she was invited to peruse. And she met Prince Alexander Bezdorodko, a man of immense wealth and high ability employed by Catherine as head of the department of

FIG. 16. *Elisabeth Vigée Le Brun*, Portrait of Prince Alexander Kurakin, *1797*. *The State Hermitage Museum, St. Petersburg.*

foreign affairs; after her death in 1796 he was made grand chancellor by Paul I, with virtual control of Russian foreign affairs (II, 67–68). He owned huge land properties with approximately thirty-thousand moujiks, peasant slaves attached to his service, whom, at least according to Vigée Le Brun's testimony, he treated with humanity, making sure, for instance, that they would be trained for various skilled trades in order to improve their chances at bettering their condition (II, 67).

It is evident from Vigée Le Brun's comments in *Souvenirs* that as an émigrée from revolutionary France she was predisposed to viewing Russian society under the most favorable light and to overlook its egregious economic and social inequalities. Indeed she was consistently eager to depict the powerful political and social rulers of Russia as benevolent and enlightened leaders who did their best to improve the conditions of the peasants, the poor, and the most disadvantaged Russians. Yet, to her credit mention should be made of the remarkable degree of independence and dignity she retained as a foreigner and self-sustained woman artist in a society hardly prepared to accommodate such an unusual personality. To be sure, her reputation as Marie-Antoinette's official portraitist had preceded her and greatly facilitated her entrée in the highest reaches of Russian society.

She could look upon this society with clear-eyed objectivity. For instance, some of the nouveaux riches she met in Moscow struck her as coarse and uncultured, and she had to attend some dinners so intolerably long and boring that she would invoke some pretext to depart before feeling truly indisposed (II, 66). On the whole, she did not derive any special pleasure from these opportunities to mingle with the most powerful and richest members of Moscow society. There were many commissions for portraits, but the persistently frigid weather eventually got the better of her; she felt ill and depressed, and decided to go back to Saint Petersburg.

It was on March 12, 1801, while Vigée Le Brun was traveling from

PLATE 9. Self-Portrait with a Straw Hat, *1783. Private collection, Switzerland. (An autograph replica is at the National Gallery, London.)*

PLATE 10. Portrait of the Duchess of Polignac, *1783*. *Waddesdon, The Roth-schild Collection (The National Trust), United Kingdom. (Photo: Pru Cuming Associates)*

PLATE 11. Marie-Antoinette and Her Children, *1787. Musée National du Château de Versailles, Versailles. (Réunion des Musées Nationaux/Art Resource, NY)*

PLATE 12. Self-Portrait with Daughter Julie, *1789*. *Musée National du Louvre, Paris. (Réunion des Musées Nationaux/Art Resource, NY)*

PLATE 13. Self-Portrait, *1790*. *Gallery of the Uffizi, Florence. (Scala/Art Resource, NY)*

PLATE 14. Self-Portrait, *1800. State Hermitage Museum, St. Petersburg. (Scala/ Art Resource, NY)*

PLATE 16. Germaine de Staël as Corinne at Cape Miseno, *1808*. © *Musée d'Art et d'Histoire, Geneva.*

Moscow to Saint Petersburg, that she learned of the death of Czar Paul I, an event that caused general popular rejoicing. When she arrived in Saint Petersburg, people were dancing in the streets, boisterously celebrating their deliverance (II, 72). Actually, Paul had been assassinated as a result of a conspiracy of the nobles and military officers dissatisfied with his rule. Vigée Le Brun asserts in *Souvenirs* that she had it from the best sources that Alexander I, Paul's son and successor, was not involved in his father's murder (II, 76). She furthermore stresses the generosity with which, contrary to the usual tradition in such circumstances, Alexander treated those who had enjoyed the favor and protection of his predecessor and, more importantly, the measures he took to free and rehabilitate his political victims, notably exiled prisoners, who were called back with their properties restored to them. In short, a promising new era seemed about to begin for Russia.

Alexander showed great personal goodwill toward Vigée Le Brun and commissioned her to paint two portraits of him, one as a bust and the other on horseback (II, 79). Equestrian portraits had never been part of her repertoire. But more importantly, she had an overwhelming need of rest and of breathing in a warmer climate, and had resolved to leave Russia. Furthermore, the efforts in her behalf in France had finally borne fruit, and on June 5, 1800, her name was stricken from the list of émigrés. She could now return to France whenever she wished to do so. This development in her favor was hardly surprising in light of the dramatic political changes that had taken place during the intervening years.

The Reign of Terror, a strong central government organized by the Committee of Public Safety, had begun with the execution of Louis XVI on January 21, 1793, and that of Marie-Antoinette on October 16, 1793. The news of their imprisonment and execution had deeply affected Vigée Le Brun, overwhelming her with an acute sense of grief and even guilt at enjoying the amenities of Russian court life while the king and queen of France, who had shown her such kindness and generosity, had become the primary victims of the Terror (II, 11).

For a staunch Royalist like Vigée Le Brun, this public regicide turned into something of a personal obsession. She even contemplated painting a historical composition representing the royal couple "in one of the touching and solemn moments preceding their death" (II, 11). But she gave up this project when she received a detailed eyewitness, and heart-rending account of the last days of Louis XVI and Marie-Antoinette by Jean-Baptiste Cléry, valet of the king who had since managed to flee to Vienna (II, 11–16). She realized that "every stroke of the brush would have caused me to dissolve into tears" (II, 16), but perhaps she also subconsciously perceived that historical painting had never been her forte and understandably recoiled from tackling such a challenging genre under these particularly trying circumstances.[18]

By 1800 Vigée Le Brun could realistically consider the possibility of returning to her homeland without any fear of personal reprisal resulting from her close association with the Old Regime. The widespread guillotining and violence of the Reign of Terror now belonged to the past, marked by the downfall of Robespierre and the coup d'état of 9 Thermidor (July 27, 1794).[19] Until 1800 France was ruled by a Directory, which strongly reacted against the Jacobin radical ideas of democracy in favor of a bourgeois liberalism. Meanwhile, however, the weak and corrupt leaders of the Directory were superseded by the young and ambitious general Bonaparte, who returned triumphantly as the "man of the hour" from military campaigns in northern Italy and Egypt. On 18 Brumaire (November 9–10, 1799), a coup d'état overthrew the Directory, and the Consulate was set up with Bonaparte as First Consul with practically unlimited personal power. This marked the end of the Revolution proper. From 1800 to 1815 Napoleon Bonaparte would hold the center of the European stage.[20]

All these personal and political factors contributed to Vigée Le

Brun's decision to leave Russia with the intention of eventually returning to France. In spite of the considerable financial and other rewards
new commissions would have brought her had she decided to remain
in Russia, she was determined to focus on her own immediate physical and emotional state which, according to doctors, required that she
take the waters at Karlsbad, a famous spa and health resort in Bohemia
whose hot mineral waters attracted European aristocracy until well after
World War I (II, 79).

To take leave of her daughter and close friends turned out to be a
distressing experience. Everyone, even Tsar Alexander and his wife,
entreated her to remain in Russia, assuring her that a good rest would
take care of her problem (II, 81). Upon reaching the Russian border she
burst into tears: "I wanted to retrace my journey, I vowed I would come
back to those who had for so long heaped upon me tokens of friendship and whose memory is forever engraved in my heart. But one must
believe in destiny, since I have never revisited the country I still regard
as my second motherland" (II, 81).

Vigée Le Brun's stay in Russia was an exceptionally productive one,
for it generated more than fifty portraits.[21] By the same token she had
a significant impact on Russian portraiture as a genre in which native
painters would excel in their own right.

CHAPTER ELEVEN

Homeward Bound

ACCOMPANIED BY the ever loyal Auguste Rivière (her sister-in-law's brother), who had faithfully followed her in her peripatetic career all the way to Russia, Vigée Le Brun was in a state of physical and emotional exhaustion as she embarked on her lengthy and arduous voyage back to Western Europe. But she gradually recovered as she eagerly took in the new sights afforded to her in the course of her journey.

Her first stop was Narva, a well-fortified little town in Estonia, edged with picturesque houses and English gardens, the Baltic sea within view. She noted that both men and women were good-looking, with women wearing colorful native costumes and men reminding her of Raphael's heads of Christ. During her stop she even took time out to sketch a nearby spectacular waterfall, for she had always been fascinated by cataracts and quite often included them in the background of her portraits. In her drawing she endeavored to capture the powerful torrent swiftly and noisily cascading against enormous rocks (II, 83). In this respect, her aesthetic sensibility was attuned to that of other pre-Romantics who extolled the so-called sublime or terrifying features of nature.[1]

Arriving in Riga, she briefly enjoyed the sights of this bustling port on the Baltic but hastened to reach Mittau, where she had learned that some members of the royal family, notably the future Louis XVIII, brother of the ill-fated Louis XVI and then known as the Count of Provence, had found refuge. Vigée Le Brun was deeply disappointed to learn upon her arrival that he and his retinue had just left the city. This failure to reconnect with the royal family plunged her once more in a debilitating state of depression. No longer interested in the passing scenery she refused to leave her carriage until finally reaching Berlin at the end of July 1801.

She soon recovered enough to accept a request from Queen Louise of Prussia, wife of Frederick William III, to go to Potsdam in order to paint her portrait. The stay in Potsdam turned out to be beneficial for Vigée Le Brun's morale and still fragile state of health. Queen Louise, a fierce opponent of the French Revolution, warmly welcomed an artist so closely associated with Marie-Antoinette, and Vigée Le Brun, in turn, was won over by her sitter's beauty and graciousness. While the painter's account of her hostess's beauty is probably not exaggerated, the praise she heaps on her character and "virtue," while understandable, is comparable to her idealized depiction of Marie-Antoinette, and she is equally eloquent in defending both women against accusations of sexual misconduct.

Berlin offered Vigée Le Brun many pleasures and distractions during her six-month stay in this city, and she greatly benefited from the protection of the powerful Hohenzollern princely family. She executed several portraits of members of that family, notably that of the lovely Princess Louisa Radzivil, née Hohenzollern, with whom she struck up a friendship, and whose husband was an accomplished harpist. She also experienced the keen satisfaction of being elected a member of the Berlin Academy of Painting and of receiving a visit of the Director of the Academy, who went out of his way in order to present her in person with a diploma officially testifying to this election (II, 91). It is worth noting that most of the portraits she executed in Berlin were in pastel, and it has been suggested that this was due to the fact that she had not yet completely recovered from her recent state of depression and exhaustion. On the other hand, it may have been a deliberate choice on her part as an artist. A similar choice had already been made by first-rate eighteenth-century painters with whose fine pastel portraits she was thoroughly familiar, notably those of Chardin and Quentin La Tour.

While in Berlin she also met personalities from the world of literature and the arts, writers, as well as actors and actresses, and it especially touched her that she was warmly received by women of letters who had achieved renown as novelists in the tradition of Rousseau's *La Nouvelle Héloïse*, notably Juliane Von Krudener, author of such best-selling novels as *Valérie*, typical of the pre-Romantic emphasis on sexual passion and on problems of relationships between men and women, as well as Adélaïde de Souza, whose epistolary novel *Adèle de Sénange* recounted the dramatic consequences of an ill-matched marriage between a sixteen-year-old girl and a seventy-year-old man (II, 90–1).[2]

Yet, in spite of the warm reception that greeted her in Berlin, Vigée Le Brun yearned increasingly to return to France. Her husband, brother, and friends had worked mightily in order to get her name removed from the list of émigrés, and on July 26, 1799, a petition on her behalf had been presented to the Directory, signed by two hundred and fifty artists and writers (including revolutionaries), among whom were such notable names as Jacques-Louis David, Jean-Baptiste Greuze, Jean-Antoine Houdon, Joseph Vernet, Hubert Robert, Jean-Honoré Fragonard, and Anne Vallayer-Coster.

Vigée Le Brun's name was finally removed from the list of émigrés on June 5, 1800. But it would not be until approximately a year later, in Berlin, that she would receive all the necessary documents authorizing her to return to France. All this would have been impossible without the intervention of the all-powerful Jacques-Louis David. After twelve years of exile, she was weary of this constant wandering and deeply yearned to return home and reconnect with her roots. At the same time, however, she had mixed feelings about the prospect of returning to Paris, for she realized that it would be an altogether very different place from the one she had so precipitously left in 1789. Her homeland had undergone profound political upheavals in her absence. Absolute monarchy had been toppled, followed by the struggle for power between the Girondins and the Montagnards, and culminating in the brief and bloody triumph of the Jacobins. Now, after his coup d'état of November 9–10, 1799, which had overthrown the Directory, General Bonaparte's star was on the rise and he had assumed power as First Consul.[3] A sense of order and strong leadership seemed to have returned to France, which appeared like a propitious time for Vigée Le Brun's return to her homeland.

Vigée Le Brun had become so accustomed to the warm hospitality extended to her by the most privileged European circles that she was understandably anxious about the kind of reception she should expect in the uncertain and unstable climate of postrevolutionary France. More-over, painful images of violence and bloodshed, notably the terrible death of Marie-Antoinette, came back to haunt her. In a letter to her brother, written in Dresden in September 1801, she confided her fears and misgivings: "I cannot hide from you what goes on in my poor head and heart at the thought of returning to Paris. As I draw closer to France, the memory of the horrors that occurred there comes back so vividly that I dread seeing again places that witnessed these dreadful scenes" (II, 94).

Even the unpleasantness she had experienced as a young victim of slanderous rumors spread by envious male painters in prerevolutionary France was recalled in contrast with the warm reception accorded her throughout Europe. Indeed, she was now in greater demand than ever: "Since I left Russia, I have been invited to Vienna, Brunswick, Munich, and London, without mentioning Saint Petersburg, where they are insistently calling me back and that I so hoped to see again; everywhere I met with the warmest and most flattering hospitality; everywhere I found a homeland" (II, 95).

Vigée Le Brun made brief stopovers in Dresden, Brunswick, and Weimar, where she spent only one day, probably unaware of the fact that it was about to become an important cultural center not only associated with Goethe, Schiller, and Romanticism, but also with Germaine de Staël and her circle in 1803. The two women would eventually meet for the first time in person only in September of 1808, at Coppet in Switzerland, where Vigée Le Brun would paint the famous portrait of the writer represented as Corinne, the heroine of her latest novel, published in 1807, *Corinne, ou l'Italie* (see plate 16).

In Gotha, capital of the old duchy of Saxe-Gotha, she was pleased to meet and renew her old acquaintance with Friedrich Melchior Grimm, who was very helpful in dealing with financial and other matters (II, 98). For about three decades Grimm had been a loyal friend of the Encyclopedists and especially of Diderot and, as editor of the influential *Correspondance Littéraire,* which had among its subscribers some of the most powerful crowned heads of Europe, notably Frederic II and Catherine II, played a key role for at least three decades in disseminating the ideas of the Enlightenment throughout Europe.[4] He had nevertheless become estranged from his friends even before the advent of the Revolution, when Diderot detected that his political and diplomatic ambitions superseded his loyalty to the cause of the Enlightenment. After the Revolution he chose the path of exile and when he and Vigée Le Brun met again he was an aging figure whose fame had been essentially associated with prerevolutionary France but who managed to conceal his personal bitterness over his fading repute behind a gracious facade.

Vigée Le Brun's anxiety and contradictory mixture of emotions increased as she neared the frontier of her homeland after a twelve-year enforced absence: "I shall not attempt to depict what I experienced as I set foot on the soil of France, which I had left twelve years earlier. Fear, pain, joy gripped me simultaneously (for there was a mixture of all this in the thousand sensations that overwhelmed my soul). I wept over friends I had lost on the scaffold; but I was going to see again those who had survived. This France, to which I was returning, had been the scene of atrocious crimes; but this France was my homeland!" (II, 100).

On January 18, 1802, she found herself once more in Paris, about to enter the house on the rue de Cléry, where she was greeted with tears of joy by her brother, sister-in-law, and even her ex-husband, who had gone out of his way to highlight this welcome by having the house lavishly decorated with flowers and other embellishments, although, as she ruefully points out in her autobiography, she eventually had to pay for this testimony out of her own pocket (II, 101). In spite of the divorce (which had been primarily dictated by political necessity) and the personal grudges Vigée Le Brun held against her spendthrift husband, the couple had obviously arrived at a mutually beneficial working relationship, and Le Brun had, after all, gone out of his way, sometimes at his own risk, to defend his wife's reputation, honor, and interests during her years of exile. No wonder, therefore, that for all kinds of practical reasons she decided to resume living in the spacious house on the rue de Cléry, which connected through a garden with a house facing the rue du Gros Chenet that also belonged to Le Brun.

On the very evening of Vigée Le Brun's arrival a concert was given in her honor in the elegant salon of the house on the rue de Cléry (normally used as a salesroom by Le Brun in his art dealings). As she entered the room she burst into tears when she was greeted by the loud applause of the audience and by the musicians tapping on their violins with their bows. But in spite of her strong emotion, as a portraitist of beautiful women, she immediately caught sight of the stunningly handsome Madame Tallien, wife of a former revolutionary politician and rabid Jacobin who, probably under her moderating influence, played a key role in the coup d'état of 9 Thermidor (July 27, 1794) that overthrew Robespierre and who subsequently became a leader in the Thermidorian reaction.[5] Madame Tallien was born Theresa Cabarrus, of Spanish parentage. She hosted a famous salon and originated the neo-Greek feminine style of dress of the Directoire period. The two women became quite friendly, although Vigée Le Brun never painted her portrait.

Vigée Le Brun's first visitor on the morrow of her arrival was Greuze, who had always been her enthusiastic supporter. She was very glad to see him, greatly touched by his testimony of enduring friendship, and noted that he had hardly aged since their last encounter, with the same abundant locks of hair framing his still youthful features (II, 102). Yet Greuze was seventy-seven years old by 1802 and had not fared well financially during the Revolution as well as a result of an acrimonious divorce from his beautiful but notoriously fickle wife, with a large settlement in her favor. Madame Greuze had frequently posed for her husband. Before her marriage she was known as Mademoiselle Babuti and ran a bookshop, where she delighted such steady customers as Diderot with her good looks.[6]

Greuze had joined the revolutionary cause by associating himself with the Commune Générale des Arts, dominated by Jacques-Louis David. But his style of genre painting, combining a moralistic message with sentimental and erotic touches, which had especially endeared him to Diderot, was no longer in favor, and the end of the Revolution found him in dire financial straits.[7] He had nevertheless reappeared in the Salon of 1800, reminding the public of his existence and meeting with a generally sympathetic reception.[8] In 1804, one year before his death, he exhibited a masterful self-portrait which highlights his commanding presence and self-confidence, and his strong, expressive features framed by the curly hair referred to by Vigée Le Brun, although she had not mentioned the fact that it had turned white, as the self-portrait attests.[9]

In spite of their ideological differences Vigée Le Brun and Greuze had remained good friends through these turbulent times, primarily because of their mutual passionate commitment to art and Greuze's strong and long-standing support of her endeavors as an artist. No wonder, therefore, that he was one of the signatories of the petition to allow her to return to France. While she was primarily a self-taught artist, she had learned a great deal from Greuze and was therefore all the more pleased to reestablish contact with him. Another early visitor among artists was her old friend Hubert Robert, who had made a name for himself for his majestic and evocative landscapes with ancient ruins and whose portrait, which she had painted in 1788 (Louvre), ranks among her most inspired works (see plate 2). Hubert Robert had been imprisoned during the Terror and had barely escaped the guillotine, but he had managed to paint "at least fifty pictures and do a great number of watercolors and drawings in his cell."[10] She duly paid her respects to Joseph-Marie Vien, dean of the neoclassical style of painting, then eighty-two years old, whom she credits for bringing about the classical revival in French art by introducing the Greek and Roman style of dress in historical painting. He received her most graciously and demonstrated that he was still artistically creative by showing her his latest sketches (II, 109).

Vigée Le Brun was eager to acquaint herself with the new generation of artists, notably François Gérard, Antoine Gros, and Anne-Louis Girodet. She singled out Gérard for a personal visit and found him most congenial. Understandably, however, she made no effort to reestablish personal contact with Jacques-Louis David, Vien's most famous pupil, doubtless because of the prominent role he played during the Revolution.[11] Her relationship with David was a complicated one, as her "Portrait à la plume" vividly attests (II, 248–50). He had occasionally frequented her salon before 1789 but seemed to subscribe to the campaign of slander that had been mounted against her. Yet even during the Terror he willingly acknowledged her superior talent. But she held him personally responsible for the imprisonment of Hubert Robert and other artists during the Terror, and therefore refused to see him when she learned upon her return to France that he wished to meet with her (II, 250). She doubtless never saw the by now famous sketch David drew of a shockingly aged Marie-Antoinette sitting proudly in a tumbril on the way to the guillotine, an image that sharply contrasts with her portraits of the ill-fated queen in all her youthful and feminine beauty (see fig. 11).

She was touched by the heart-warming visits that other old friends and acquaintances paid her in the days following her return to Paris, and attended some elegant balls, frequented by all the new notables and beautiful women. Even the Comédie Française, remembering her keen interest in the theater, not only offered her free passes to its performances, but also let her know through her brother, Etienne, that their foremost actors would welcome the opportunity to give a performance in her salon (II, 105). It was as though this warm welcome on the part of her compatriots was meant to make up for all the dire accusations and calumnies that had been hurled at her in the intervening years. One of her first outings was to the Louvre, which had been enriched by the spoils of Bonaparte's victorious campaigns in Italy. She visited it by herself in order to enjoy the masterpieces without any extraneous distraction but lingered so long that she failed to heed the warnings of the guards and found herself locked in after closing time. Only her desperate shouts and repeated vigorous knocks on doors eventually brought about her liberation (II, 105).

On the whole, however, Vigée Le Brun felt a pervading sense of unease and estrangement in postrevolutionary Paris, for everything around her reminded her of the political, social, and artistic upheavals that had taken place during her absence. To be sure, by the time she had returned to Paris the bloodshed and Terror associated with Robespierre had been replaced by the Directoire in 1795 and by the meteoric rise of

Bonaparte. The French capital had emerged from these dramatic events somewhat shabby but generally fairly unscathed. Yet Paris struck Vigée Le Brun as less cheerful and lively and seemed to have lost its sense of elegance of splendor. The streets appeared narrower than she had remembered them, and she was jolted to see the words "Liberty, Fraternity or Death!" scribbled on many walls: "These words, sanctified by the Terror, aroused the saddest thoughts in me about the past, and inspired some fear in me about the future" (II, 106). Crossing for the first time the former Place Louis XV, renamed Place de la Révolution and then Place de la Concorde, where the guillotine had been erected and so many executions had taken place, she was overtaken by a feeling of dread and still seemed to see the ghosts of the noble victims stoically going to their death, notably her generous royal patroness, Marie-Antoinette. Even when attending for the first time a performance at the Comédie Française, the audience looked exceedingly dull to her. Accustomed as she had been, in France and abroad, to seeing men with powdered hair and brilliant dress, the sight of a sea of dark heads and somber clothes made a depressing picture. One would have thought that this was a funereal rather than a theatrical event (II, 106). Women's fashion, on the other hand, was far more colorful and daring, for it had been overtaken by the classicizing predilection for high-waisted, flowing dresses and tunics in diaphanous and revealing fabrics, such as white muslin, that evoked the simple and more "natural" Roman style. Elaborate coiffures and enormous hooped skirts had vanished, replaced by a far softer, more "natural" look which highlighted and sometimes even exposed women's bosoms.

Vigée Le Brun soon discovered that her initial impression of the French capital as having lost its prerevolutionary social brilliance was somewhat erroneous as she renewed old acquaintances and made some new ones, notably that of Madame Récamier, a great beauty immortalized in portraits by François Gérard and, especially, Jacques-Louis

David, and famous for her friendships with Chateaubriand and Germaine de Staël. As the wife of a rich banker, Madame Récamier had the financial means to organize glittering social events, and one of her great balls proved to Vigée Le Brun that Old Regime splendor and luxury had not altogether been superseded by the plebeian street dances known as the "carmagnoles." Only one other woman could rival with Madame Récamier with respect to beauty, and that was Madame Tallien. Always sensitive to feminine beauty, Vigée Le Brun was especially taken by her stunning good looks, for she found her to be at once "beautiful and pretty," a rare combination of classical regularity of features and appealing expressiveness. Madame Tallien was not only beautiful, she also had great generosity of heart, for as the wife of the powerful Tallien she managed to save a number of lives at the height of the Terror through the moderating influence she exerted on her husband.

The Revolution was definitely over, and a fever of pleasure seemed to have overtaken the French capital. There were balls everywhere, theaters had reopened, and plays as well as operas were attended by packed audiences. A class of nouveaux riches that had profiteered from recent events had risen to the fore and was eager to flaunt ostentatiously its wealth and power. Those who had most benefited from the revolutionary wars and Bonaparte's campaigns were bankers who had charged enormous interest rates, purveyors of food and provisions for the armies, and all manner of speculators.[12] The Tuileries Palace, chosen residence of Napoleon Bonaparte and his beautiful wife, Joséphine, had replaced the now empty and abandoned Versailles as a courtly center of social life.

Vigée Le Brun caught her first glimpse of Bonaparte, at the time First Consul, at a military parade which she viewed from one of the windows of the Louvre. She found it difficult to believe that this small, thin figure of a man being pointed out to her was indeed Bonaparte. As in the case of Catherine the Great, she had rather naively imagined that powerful people had commensurate physical proportions. Although Bonaparte's brothers paid her a courtesy visit soon after her return to Paris, and Lucien in particular expressed a flattering interest in her paintings (II, 107), her relation with the Napoleonic regime would be an uneasy and difficult one, most probably because there was deep political distrust on both sides.

In order to overcome a pervading sense of melancholy, Vigée Le Brun decided to organize soirées and balls as well as theatrical amateur events to which she invited not only French notables but also Russians and Germans who were then part of the occupying forces in Paris in order to repay them for the warm hospitality they had extended to her during her years of exile.

She did very little painting during this period and submitted previously completed works to the 1802 Salon, notably her portrait of Stanislas II Augustus, king of Poland, and a longtime personal favorite, her portrait of Lady Hamilton as a sibyl, painted in Naples in 1792, in order to reestablish herself among a new generation of up-and-coming artists. The critical reviews were generally favorable. But she continued to feel depressed in spite of her socializing and decided to try to find comfort in leaving the bustle of the French capital and seeking refuge in the country. She impulsively rented a little house in Meudon, a picturesque small town to the southwest of Paris. Situated in the midst of woods, the house, which had once served as a retreat for Capuchin monks, was sufficiently isolated to make her feel that she was a thousand miles from Paris and to provide her with the kind of quiet solitude she yearned for. Yet by the autumn of 1802 she felt restless and returned to the city, where once more she was overtaken by gloomy thoughts. In spite of its renewed glitter Paris under the Consulate reminded her too poignantly of the refined, elegant pre-1789 world peopled by the gracious ghosts of her youth.

In order to attempt to fend off this nostalgic, melancholy state of mind, she decided that a journey abroad and a total change of scenery would be in order. Travel had always revitalized her energies, and her spirits unfailingly soared whenever she visited great cities and diligently acquainted herself with their cultural and artistic treasures. She resolved to go to London, which she had never seen before (although rumors had persistently circulated to the effect that she had followed Calonne, reputedly her lover, across the Channel after fleeing from revolutionary France). Even though she did not know a word of English she was eager to familiarize herself with the British capital, its society, and its art. She also counted on her European renown, her connections, and the popularity of portraiture as a genre in England in order to find a new clientele and wealthy sitters among the nobility, since postrevolutionary Paris had not exactly showered her with commissions. She set out for London on April 15, 1803. Her timing was all the more propitious since the Peace Treaty of Amiens of 1802 had put an end, at least temporarily, to the hostilities between France and England.

CHAPTER TWELVE

❧ *The English Interlude* ❧

VIGÉE LE BRUN expected to stay a few months in England. She ended up remaining there for more than two years, until July of 1805, retained not only by professional commitments but also by the warm hospitality extended to her by the English. Besides, with its brilliant social life and thriving art market, London had a great deal to offer an enterprising, resourceful visitor like Vigée Le Brun. That she did not know the language did not present a significant obstacle, for she would move primarily in the exclusive circles of English aristocrats, who were generally conversant in French, as well as émigrés. Among her compatriots, old friends and acquaintances went out of their way to greet her and help her settle down. As the official portraitist of the martyred Marie-Antoinette, she was warmly received by the British nobility.

With the uneasy and short-lived peace following the 1802 Treaty of Amiens, relations between France and England relaxed somewhat, and a number of British aristocrats, who had not crossed the Channel since 1789, even ventured to visit Paris in order to acquaint themselves in person with Bonaparte's regime, the consular court, and the latest trends in art and fashion.[1]

Vigée Le Brun made the crossing of the Channel from Calais to

Dover accompanied by an English maid who turned out to be unreliable and had to be discharged. Luckily she had also brought along a more helpful young woman, Adélaïde, who had earned her mistress's confidence and trust. She could no longer count on the comforting presence of the loyal Auguste Rivière, and her daughter, Julie Nigris, had of course stayed with her husband in Saint Petersburg. On disembarking in Dover she hastened to hire a three-horse chaise, and as dusk was rapidly falling she felt anxious, for she had heard alarming rumors about highwaymen frequently robbing travelers. She therefore took the precaution of hiding her diamonds in her stockings. Fortunately nothing untoward happened on the journey from Dover to the English capital.

Upon her arrival in London, Vigée Le Brun stayed a while in the Hotel Brunet in Leicester Square, today a bustling tourist center in the theater district but then a relatively quiet place inhabited by such artists as William Hogarth and Joshua Reynolds. But she needed a more permanent residence. A flat on Baker Street in the West End, where many French émigrés resided, presented several annoying inconveniences, for it faced the noisy barracks and stables of the Royal Houseguards, which prevented her from sleeping, and during the daytime a neighboring family with numerous wild, unruly children made an unbearable racket. She moved to a house on elegant Portman Square, where more unpleasant surprises awaited her, even though she had taken the precaution of inspecting it beforehand. Her next-door neighbor owned a huge parrot that never stopped screeching. Already unhinged by the owner's refusal to move the bird to a part of the house farther away from her flat, she learned that the house had previously been occupied by Indian diplomats who had used the cellar as a burial place for their deceased servants. She finally settled in on Maddox Street, deciding that, in spite of its dampness, the flat was quiet and spacious enough to accommodate her studio as well as a salon for socializing.

As was her custom, once recovered from her journey and apartment hunting, she set out to explore tirelessly the vast metropolis and its surroundings and to investigate every aspect of English life that was to fall within her reach. Her natural inquisitiveness was all the more aroused since she had a great deal to learn about British society, politics, and the arts.

The English had figured prominently in the political, philosophical, and literary history of prerevolutionary France. The vast English contributions to political and economic theory, fiction, poetry, and the theater have been well documented.[2] French public opinion was decidedly pro-English, for the philosophes, notably Voltaire in his highly controversial but also immensely influential 1733 *Letters Concerning the English Nation*, had underscored the great accomplishments of Newton and Locke, the genius of Shakespeare, and had praised English religious tolerance, political structure, and commerce. Despite the Seven Years' War (1756–63), a complex struggle during which France and England struggled for supremacy, Anglomania became the new vogue among the French intellectual and enlightened elite. The English political system, with its constitutional monarchy and parliamentary traditions, came to be looked upon as a model that France would do well to imitate if she was to achieve an enlightened social system of her own.

Vigée Le Brun's relationship with the philosophes was a conflicted one. While her own political stance and close association with Marie-Antoinette precluded an overt admiration for Voltaire and the Encyclopedists, her friendship with such painters as Hubert Robert and especially Jean-Baptiste Greuze, so closely associated with Diderot, and her obvious familiarity with the works of Rousseau suggest that she was closer to those controversial writers than she cared to admit. In this context, it is revealing to find among her lively pen portraits ("portraits à la plume") appended to her autobiographical *Souvenirs* a sympathetic sketch of Voltaire, whose triumphal return to Paris in 1778 was consecrated by a performance of his play *Irène* at the Comédie Française on

March 30 of that year, an apotheosis during which, in his presence, his bust was placed on the stage and crowned with a laurel wreath to the thunderous applause of the audience.[3] Vigée Le Brun attended this ceremony and vividly describes it as well as the famous old man who was by then so frail that she feared such strong emotions would kill him. She was even strongly tempted to pay him a personal visit, but gave up the idea when she learned that the numerous admirers who insisted on seeing him left him in a state of total exhaustion (II, 322). And indeed, Voltaire died shortly thereafter, on May 30, 1778. But it is obvious that Vigée Le Brun viewed Voltaire as a celebrity rather than as a leader of the Enlightenment movement. She had no ideological reason for subscribing to Anglomania. Her views and opinions on English customs and manners were therefore generally spontaneous and of a personal nature.

She admired the broad and generally clean thoroughfares of London, which, with their sidewalks were so convenient for pedestrians and contrasted favorably with the narrow Paris streets, but she felt repulsed by the fairly frequent spectacle of men engaged in fierce boxing matches, surrounded by enthusiastic onlookers handing them glasses of gin to stimulate their energy (II, 121). She visited St. Paul's Cathedral and deemed its massive dome an imitation of St. Peter's in Rome (II, 121). She also made it a point to visit the Tower of London and Westminster Abbey, duly pausing before the tombs of English kings and queens, especially that of the ill-fated Mary Stuart, and she also lingered in the Poets' Corner before the memorials to great English writers and poets, notably Milton, Shakespeare, Pope, and Chatterton. The latter had by then become a symbol of the Romantic genius victim of an indifferent society that allowed him to starve to the point of committing suicide, whereas, in Vigée Le Brun's words, "the money used to render him this posthumous honor would have sufficed to provide him with a good sustenance while he was alive" (II, 121).

Social life in London, she observed with some amused puzzlement, differed markedly from that in Paris, and she found it generally on the dull side: "Sundays in London are as depressing as the climate. Not a single shop is open; there are no plays, no balls, no concerts. General silence reigns everywhere; and as on that day no one is allowed to work or even allowed to play music without risking having his windows shattered by the populace, there is no other resource, to pass the time, but public promenades, which were indeed very popular" (II, 122). Londoners tended to promenade in solemn silence, segregated according to gender. Generally dressed in white, women were so quiet and demure that they might be taken for perambulating ghosts. Yet she soon discovered that social life in London could be quite animated. Londoners frequented such public parks as Ranelagh and Vauxhall, where they could enjoy balls, fireworks, and other distractions. Among other amusements there were concerts, prominently featuring Haydn, for the elite, horse racing for the fashionable, and brutal boxing matches for the common folk.

Vigée Le Brun was naturally eager to visit art collections and acquaint herself with the English school of painting. She was disappointed to learn that, unlike Paris and other European capitals, London did not have museums, for indeed the National Gallery, the Tate Gallery, and the Wallace Collection did not yet exist.[4] She saw mostly the natural history collections then housed in Montagu House, which hardly excited her. It was only in 1845 that Montagu House was torn down and replaced by the imposing and far more capacious British Museum.[5] Great works of art were generally inaccessible to the public, for they largely belonged to the royal family and the nobility and hung on the walls of royal castles and palaces.

Vigée Le Brun would soon be warmly welcomed into the highest spheres of British society. One of her most ardent admirers was the rakish Prince of Wales, son of George III and future George IV, who not only faithfully attended her musical soirées but also commissioned a full-length portrait of himself in military uniform and welcomed her to view his extensive collection of paintings. That the future king of England should have selected a French artist to paint his portrait seems to have aroused the hostility on the part of English painters, notably that of the English portraitist John Hoppner. He authored a sharply critical appraisal of the French "school" of painting and "its frigid productions" in general and of Vigée Le Brun in particular for "the mediocrity of her talents" and for having the effrontery of charging "thrice the sum" for her portraits than that charged by the great Sir Joshua Reynolds himself.[6] She promptly responded with a letter vigorously defending the whole school of French artists, from Simon Vouet to Jacques-Louis David, and by the same token her own style of painting (II, 132–34).

Vigée Le Brun gives of the Prince of Wales a vivid and sympathetic portrait. She depicts him as a man in his forties, already quite portly, tall and handsome, with regular features, an idol of women, and fully conversant in French, and even alludes to his scandalous love life and to his secret marriage with the Roman Catholic Maria Anne Fitzherbert, "a widow older than he but extremely beautiful" (II, 131). The future George IV, unlike his earnest and lackluster parents, was a colorful, even scandalous character. A passionate lover of beauty, fashion, and parties, he was also a reckless gambler who accumulated immense debts. Carlton House was his luxurious London residence where he lavishly entertained. He also initiated the building of the Royal Pavilion in Brighton, the new trendy resort that was an extravagant architectural ensemble combining Indian and Moorish styles.[7]

Vigée Le Brun was eager to acquaint herself with the English style of painting and, making it a point to visit artists in their studios, was amused to learn that in England it was customary to charge an admission fee. On the whole she was greatly impressed by their coloristic qualities but expressed reservations about what she termed their "unfinished" style (II, 123).

The first studio she visited was that of Benjamin West, an American-born artist who had made his reputation in England as a history painter. There she saw several compositions that greatly impressed her, even though they were as yet unfinished (II, 123). That she liked his manner of painting is hardly surprising, for both as a history painter and as a portraitist West deftly mingled neoclassical and Romantic styles and demonstrated great versatility, earning him an international reputation. His London studio, located in a fine mansion, was thronged by all manner of visitors. He was appointed Historical Painter to George III, who commissioned a series of Biblical scenes, and he eventually replaced Joshua Reynolds as president of the Royal Academy, even though Reynolds had expressed serious reservations about his style of painting. More significantly, in the context of the development of American art he built a bridge between American and European painting, and his studio attracted such promising young American artists as Gilbert Stuart.[8]

The English painter with whom Vigée formed the closest personal and professionally useful relationship was Sir Joshua Reynolds. He was her strongest advocate in England by openly declaring his admiration for her portraits, and as president of the Royal Academy his opinion carried a great deal of weight. For her part, she visited his studio numerous times, admired him as a colorist and found that his compositions reminded her of Titian. Yet she deemed his paintings "generally rather unfinished, with the exception of the heads" (II, 123), a criticism she leveled at English artists in general. This reservation reflects a fundamental aspect of Vigée Le Brun's own aesthetics. A strong believer in the importance of coloristic values in the tradition of Rubens, she paid enormous attention to colors in her own compositions, but at the same time felt the necessity to work carefully on those details and accessories that she deemed essential to the overall effect.

Vigée Le Brun never mentions the name of Turner in her *Souvenirs*, yet by an interesting coincidence he had been elected to the Royal

Academy in 1802, the same year she came to England.[9] It is most likely that she never met the foremost English romantic painter and most original landscape artist, for he led a generally solitary and recluse existence, so unlike Vigée Le Brun's deliberate social visibility. Neither does she mention the name of Constable, even though this great landscape painter first exhibited at the Royal Academy in 1802.[10] Similarly, she fails to acknowledge Lawrence, a prodigiously talented portraitist who would eventually succeed Benjamin West as president of the Royal Academy in 1820.[11] Both Constable and Lawrence would exhibit and gain official recognition as well as the admiration of such forward-looking French artists as Delacroix at the Paris 1824 Salon, despite the persistent hostility on the part of some French critics.

Vigée Le Brun's reticence with respect to these great artists probably reflects her general reservation toward the "unfinished" technique of English artists. Her own style and predilection for such masters of color as Rubens might have predisposed her to Turner, Constable, and Lawrence, but she evidently made no special effort to acquaint herself with their work, probably because their reputation had not yet been fully established and, humbly born, they were not part of the exalted English aristocratic social circles she frequented. Turner's father was a barber, Constable's a miller, and Lawrence's an innkeeper.

In keeping with a practice she had established early on in her career, Vigée Le Brun felt it incumbent upon her to give elegant musical soirées in her spacious flat on Maddox Street featuring either notable opera singers or virtuosos of the violin and attended by members of the most exclusive circles of English society including, at times, the Prince of Wales himself. As an artist with an astute business sense, she correctly surmised that such socializing was necessary to sustain the goodwill and interest of her powerful and influential English patrons.

One of the visits Vigée Le Brun received was that of the notorious Emma Hamilton, whom she had known in Naples and portrayed as a ravishingly seductive sibyl. By now, however, the recently widowed Lady Hamilton had become enormously fat. Dressed in deep mourning, her features shrouded by an immense black veil, she tearfully said that she would never get over the loss of Sir William. Yet she continued her amorous correspondence with her famous lover, according to Vigée Le Brun who, upon paying her a visit one day, found her in a state of ecstatic joy because she had recently received a letter from Lord Nelson (I, 203). Remembering Emma Hamilton's highly successful performances as an artist of "attitudes," which had contributed to her enormous popularity in Naples, Vigée Le Brun agreed to devote one of her soirées to such a spectacle. The result was quite impressive, for Emma Hamilton managed, in spite of her girth, to assume "various attitudes with a truly admirable expression. . . . She went from sorrow to joy, from joy to dread, so well and with such swiftness that we were all amazed" (I, 204). Later Vigée Le Brun learned that Emma Hamilton had ended her days in Calais in a state of "abject misery" (I, 204).

During her stay in England Vigée Le Brun not only renewed her friendship with a number of notable French émigrés, she also won over, with her vivacious personality and charm, her English sitters who invited her to their homes and country estates. She took advantage of every opportunity to escape from London, whose climate she found not only depressing but even unhealthy. On the other hand, she loved the English countryside and admired its magnificent parks and gardens. She visited Windsor Castle and its great park, and Hampton Court Palace, where she admired the Raphael cartoons (now in the Victoria and Albert Museum).

She also visited Brighton, the nearest south coast resort to London, which had become fashionable in the mid-eighteenth century and was patronized by the Prince of Wales, who had established residence there and had the Royal Pavilion built in the style of a lavish oriental palace. She took long, delightful walks alongside the sea, where she could perceive the coast of France. Indeed the English, fearing an imminent invasion of the French led by Napoleon, had gathered a large army in Brighton. But for a French foreigner like Vigée Le Brun, the patriotic fervor that gripped the English nation was dismissed merely as an inconvenient military presence with generals unceasingly reviewing the National Guard, and a lot of noisy drum beating (II, 141).[12]

A visit to Bath was also de rigueur—the most elegant and fashionable English spa resort. A letter to her brother, dated February 12, 1803, gives a full account of Vigée Le Brun's three-week stay there, focusing primarily on its social rituals in descriptions that evoke *Northanger Abbey*, although she most probably never met Jane Austen (II, 141–44), who at that time had not yet published any of her novels and was not the kind of celebrity that would have attracted public attention. On the whole, however, she found life in England rather bland and "monotonous," especially in comparison with Paris and Saint Petersburg (II, 148). Yet she felt so warmly welcomed by the English that it made her forget the constant fog that enveloped London, and she would have prolonged her stay there were it not for letters from France that informed her that her daughter, Julie, was back in Paris.

CHAPTER THIRTEEN

❧ *Return to Imperial France* ❧

WHEN VIGÉE LE BRUN left France in 1803, it was under the Consulate. When she decided to return to her homeland in 1805, it was under
the Empire. In the meantime, Bonaparte had consolidated his power
by proclaiming himself Emperor of the French in May 1804 before a
subservient senate. After confirmation by a plebiscite on December 2,
1804, in a solemn ceremony at the Cathedral of Notre Dame in Paris,
he seized the crown from the hands of Pope Pius VII and placed it on
his own head, thereby proclaiming the French Empire as a uniquely
personal achievement that he owed to no one but himself. It was followed
by many public celebrations in the French capital.[1] Napoleon's apogee is
depicted by Jacques-Louis David in an enormous and theatrical composition titled *Le Sacre de Joséphine* (Louvre). It had been decided that
it would be politically prudent not to depict the moment when Napoleon
crowned himself, but rather when he places the crown on Josephine's
head.[2]

It was with some reluctance that Vigée Le Brun left England, where
she had met with warm hospitality and had formed many friendships:
"I have often heard that the English are not hospitable; I don't share

this opinion, and am very grateful for the reception that was accorded to me in London" (II, 152).

A primary reason for Vigée Le Brun's decision to return to France was that her daughter, Julie, and her husband had left Russia and were now in Paris. Nigris had been entrusted by Prince Narishkin with the mission of engaging French artists for the Imperial Theater of Saint Petersburg. Soon after their arrival in the French capital, however, Nigris returned to his homeland by himself, leaving his wife in the lurch, an action that confirmed Vigée Le Brun's poor opinion of her son-in-law's character. Mother and daughter had not seen each other in five years.

Because of the renewed hostilities between France and England she had to set sail for Rotterdam rather than a French port, where she was detained for a fortnight before being allowed to proceed to her destination. She reached Paris in July of 1805 and settled once more at the Hôtel Le Brun, where she would cohabit on fairly amicable terms with her ex-husband. The joy of being reunited with her daughter, with whom she had been estranged in Russia following Julie's ill-fated marriage to Nigris, was of short duration. Julie still had a wild, uncontrollable streak, socialized with the wrong people, and refused to live with her mother. In one of the most candid admissions in *Souvenirs*, Vigée Le Brun touchingly acknowledges her partial failure as a mother: "Whether it is through my fault or not, her power over my mind was great, and I had none over hers, and it is therefore understandable that she sometimes made me shed bitter tears. Still, she was my daughter; her beauty, her talents, her wit made her exceedingly fascinating" (II, 155).

True to the role she had always enjoyed playing as hostess, Vigée Le Brun promptly resumed her active social life with old friends, made new ones, and gave musical and theatrical soirées at the Hôtel Le Brun, where she featured promising young singers and actresses, but where she was also pleased to receive some of the surviving members of her circle of friends of prerevolutionary France, notably her good friend and mentor the painter Hubert Robert, who, in spite of his advancing years, could still enliven the gatherings with the playfulness of a schoolboy (II, 157).

Her loyalty to the Bourbons and especially to the ill-fated Marie-Antoinette hardly prepared Vigée Le Brun to cope successfully with the regime of the new imperial ruler of France and much of Europe. While still in London she had learned of the summary execution of the Duc d'Enghien, the last surviving heir to the Bourbon-Condé who had emigrated in 1789 but was kidnapped from his residence in Etten-heim, Baden, and within a few hours court-martialed and shot in Vincennes on March 21, 1804, in order to forestall any restoration of the Bourbon monarchy. In her *Souvenirs* she notes that when news of this execution reached London it plunged the public into such consternation that it caused the performance of a play she was attending to be stopped abruptly (II, 137). The following day, she went to a solemn mass in honor of the victim, a ceremony that was attended not only by the French exiles, but also by a large number of English Bourbon sympathizers (II, 137). She was all the more affected by this news since she personally knew both the Duc d'Enghien and his father, the Duc de Bourbon, whom she had met in Turin. The Duc de Bourbon was in London at the time of his son's death, and when he paid the portraitist a visit a month thereafter, she was profoundly shocked by his appearance and demeanor: "He entered without speaking, sat down, and burying his face covered with tears with his two hands, whispered: 'No, I shall never get over it!'" (II, 137).

For his part, Napoleon had no special reason to be favorably disposed toward Marie-Antoinette's portraitist. And that she had opted to make a prolonged stay in London, the center of the opposition to France, could hardly endear her to him. And indeed, soon after her return to Paris, she learned that he had curtly remarked: "Madame Le Brun went to England to visit *her friends*" (II, 158). Yet, the Emperor's resentment did not prevent him from commissioning her in March of 1806 to execute a full-length portrait of his sister Caroline Murat, wife of Joachim Murat, king of Naples. Her loyalty to the Bourbons and especially to the ill-fated Marie-Antoinette did not dispose her favorably toward the new imperial ruler of France and of much of Europe. Yet she could hardly turn down this offer, although the financial remuneration was less than half of her customary fee, and she even decided to include in the portrait Caroline Murat's daughter Laetitia for no additional charge (II, 159).

The execution of the portrait was complicated by all kinds of annoyances principally caused by Caroline Murat's caprices, rudeness, and lack of consideration for the artist (plate 15). She would arrive late for sittings or not show up at all. She would change her hairstyle, outfit, and jewelry during the intervals between sittings, thereby repeatedly forcing her portraitist to scrape off and repaint parts of the composition. Vigée Le Brun was so irritated by her subject's poor manners that she observed in a voice loud enough to be overheard by Caroline Murat herself: "I have painted *real* princesses who have never tormented me or kept me waiting" (II, 160). This stinging comment summarized Vigée Le Brun's disdainful attitude toward the nobility of the Empire, which she never viewed as legitimate. Not too surprisingly, no further official commission would be forthcoming during the Empire.

Vigée Le Brun might have settled down, surrounded by her old and new friends, and accommodated herself to the new regime. After all, her vast experience dealing with royalty and high nobility equipped her to deal diplomatically with temperamental and unpredictable sitters. But she obviously found it difficult to resign herself to the Napoleonic rule. After two years she felt once more restive, and probably had good reasons to leave Paris in view of her barely repressed hostility toward the new regime.

She had never visited Switzerland and felt a strong urge to see for herself "a land so loved by artists, poets, and dreamers" (II, 165), and especially the mountains, lakes, and other sites made immortal by Jean-Jacques Rousseau's novel *Julie, ou La Nouvelle Héloïse*, which, like so many women of her generation, she had read with great fervor.[3] She also keenly admired Rousseau's *Confessions*, which must have played a part in the inspiration of her own autobiographical *Souvenirs*, in which his name reappears in various contexts.

Despite her fierce loyalty to the monarchy, Vigée Le Brun could not renounce intellectual and aesthetic relationships that linked her one way or another with the philosophes. Of these, Rousseau, the novelist and autobiographer rather than political theorist and social critic, had a special kind of appeal to her. She doubtless must have realized that he was hardly an idol of the Royalists, but like other émigrés and counter-revolutionaries she appreciated and even identified with Rousseau the wanderer, dreamer, and expatriate, and did not seem unduly concerned with this apparent contradiction. But then, Rousseau had the singular privilege of being either revered or execrated for reasons of personal affinity rather than ideology.[4] Shortly before the Revolution she had visited Ermenonville, where Rousseau died and had been laid to rest in 1778 (I, 119). To visit Switzerland would therefore afford her the opportunity of not only making a sentimental pilgrimage to the sites associated with the life and works of Rousseau, but more importantly to view for herself those awesome aspects of nature such as mountains, lakes, and waterfalls identified with the sublime. She had always been a worshipper of nature, had even at one time aspired to be a landscape artist. She had made serious attempts at painting landscapes directly from nature and had frequently included in her portraits vistas of lush vegetation, ancient and leafy trees, and open sky, as well as such naturally romantic and picturesque features as lofty mountains, rocks overgrown with moss, and cascading waterfalls.

Vigée Le Brun spent the summers of 1807 and 1808 in Switzerland

and gave a lively account of her two trips in nine letters, eventually incorporated in the autobiographical *Souvenirs*, addressed to Countess Helen Potocka, a Polish princess, born Massalska, widow of prince Charles-Joseph de Ligne's son, Charles de Ligne, killed in 1792 fighting against the French during the wars of the Revolution (fig. 17). Vigée Le Brun's long-standing friendship with the vastly cultured, sophisticated, and witty prince Charles-Joseph de Ligne goes a long way toward explaining the intimacy she established with his daughter-in-law.

Vigée Le Brun's letters to Countess Potocka are largely modeled after the travelogue made popular in eighteenth-century France. The voyage literature, such as the imaginary voyage, extraordinary voyage, philosophical voyage, and the like were widely used to designate a variety of narratives. Generally, however, these narratives were by male travelers. Vigée Le Brun's own narrative is distinctly couched from a feminine point of view. It assumes the form of familiar, lively letters, written by a woman to her woman friend, and offers a vivid picture of what Switzerland was like for an early nineteenth-century woman traveler. Her goal was to share with Countess Potocka the impressions she gathered "in a land so loved by artists, poets, and dreamers" and to evoke natural sites "of the greatest sublimity" (II, 165). She furthermore recorded her voyage in the form of numerous pastel landscapes which deserve serious study as a significant and heretofore overlooked aspect of her artistic production.

She first made her way from Basel to Bienne, for this itinerary had been recommended to her as particularly spectacular. But the narrow road was bordered by precipices, and when the horse drawing her carriage unexpectedly stumbled she nearly fell into the abyss. Reaching the Ile de Saint-Pierre, on the Lake of Bienne, where Rousseau had found a refuge from persecution from his own compatriots and a measure of serenity in 1765, so poetically evoked in the *Reveries of the Solitary*

FIG. 17. *Elisabeth Vigée Le Brun*, Portrait of Countess Potocka, *1791*. *Private collection*, *U.S.A. (Courtesy of Stiebel, ltd.)*

Walker (Rêveries du promeneur solitairer), she paused at length in order to savor fully the pastoral scene. She was shocked, however, to find that the little house Rousseau had inhabited on Ile de Saint-Pierre had been converted into a tavern and duly expressed her outrage: "The immortal renown of the Genevan writer could not save his home from this profanation!" (II, 164).

Vigée Le Brun made sure to visit other sites associated with the life and works of Rousseau, noting wryly the hostility with which his own compatriots had at first greeted the idea of erecting a statue in his honor in his native city and adding, "This great writer is generally detested in Geneva" (II, 186). Rousseau was very much on her mind when she took the boat trip on Lake Geneva in honor of Julie and Saint-Preux, the tragic protagonists of *La Nouvelle Héloïse:* "My boat was alone on the lake; the vast silence that surrounded me was troubled only by the light sound of the oars. I fully savored a brilliant and beautiful moon; a few silvery clouds followed it in the sky. The lake was so calm, so transparent that the moon and these lovely clouds reflected in it as in a mirror" (II, 180). The sentiments evoked here faithfully reflect those of a whole generation of Romantic writers, from Lamartine to Byron, for whom Lake Geneva and its environs embodied an ideal but doomed love story that took place in the picturesque setting of the Swiss landscape.

A highlight of Vigée Le Brun's Swiss trips was the visit she paid to Germaine de Staël at Coppet in September 1808, which inspired her to paint de Staël's portrait as the heroine of the novel, *Corinne*, published that same year to much acclaim, notoriety, and controversy. Although the two women came from different social backgrounds and acquired their fame in different media, the trajectory of their lives and careers presents some striking parallels. Both women had demonstrated a remarkably precocious talent in their respective fields of endeavor; both were disappointed in their quest to find happiness and personal fulfillment in marriage and motherhood; and both found in Rousseau an unparalleled opportunity for self-revelation. After reading his writings, they dared to expect something more from life than self-abnegation in the performance of their duties as wives and mothers. Like so many other women readers, they intuitively regarded him as that rare, sensitive soul capable of comprehending their innermost needs and aspirations.[5]

By today's standards, Rousseau's sexual politics appear blatantly misogynistic. Yet, the paradox remains that it was Rousseau, more than any other eighteenth-century philosophe, who inspired such exceptional women as Vigée Le Brun and Staël to break free from the constraints imposed upon their sex. The philosophes were not necessarily proponents of the notion of equal rights and opportunities for women, and they were hardly willing to consider women as equals in intellect and creativity. They were nevertheless sincerely sympathetic to their plight in society but continued to view them with kindly condescension, as Diderot's eloquent yet curiously ambiguous essay *On Women (Sur les femmes)* amply demonstrates.[6]

By the time of Vigée Le Brun's visit at Coppet, Staël had become a celebrated, if controversial, figure on the European political, literary, and cultural scene, thanks to her widely read and influential works and her tireless political activism and powerful, high-profile personality. She was playing a key role as faithful inheritor of the Enlightenment legacy and as a key founder of the Romantic movement. At Coppet Vigée Le Brun also met Benjamin Constant, political writer, novelist, and Staël's lover, as well as Madame Récamier, celebrated French beauty, among the famous writer's guests.

Vigée Le Brun had read *Corinne*, and this gave her the idea of painting a portrait of its author in the guise of its tragic heroine. Against a romantic background of dark, steep mountains and dramatically lighted sky, Germaine as Corinne is shown seated on a rock, an inspired expression animating her face and uplifted eyes, her hands gracefully playing on a lyre. She is wearing a simple Grecian-like outfit consisting of a white muslin gown with a generous décolleté showing off her shoulders and arms. A red toga is loosely draped around her amply proportioned hips (plate 16).

By the painter's own admission, "Madame de Staël was not pretty" (II, 181). Even though as a portraitist Vigée Le Brun was supremely adept at bringing out appealingly feminine features in her women sitters, Staël presented something of a special challenge, for her physical appearance did not conform to the current canon of feminine beauty. By all contemporary accounts she was rather corpulent and did not have the delicate facial features then so greatly prized. The resulting portrait shows a powerful rather than a vulnerable and sexually seductive woman. It is decidedly less flattering (and probably more realistically faithful to its subject) than François Gérard's later and more lyrically idealized portrait of Staël as *Corinne au cap Misène* (fig. 18).

In order to sustain her sitter's inspired expression, Vigée Le Brun asked her to recite passages from tragedies by Corneille or Racine during the posing sessions (II, 181). Whether Staël was ultimately pleased with her portrait is impossible to tell, although in a letter to the painter's daughter she diplomatically writes that "your mother has painted me as Corinne in a portrait truly more poetic than my own work" (II, 183).

The two famous women seem to have established a warm, friendly relationship, for they had a great deal in common. Both women had paid a high price for their independence and their determination to pursue a self-sustaining, creative career. Both, furthermore, had experienced the dangers and difficulties of exile and political emigration. Napoleon's unrelenting hostility toward the author of *Corinne* could only endear her to Marie-Antoinette's loyal portraitist and friend, who had incurred the Emperor's displeasure upon her return to France from England and who had been treated rudely and inconsiderately by the Emperor's sister when she sat for her portrait.

FIG. 18. *François Gérard,* Germaine de Staël as Corinne at Cape Miseno, *1822. Musée des Beaux-Arts, Lyons.*

In *Souvenirs* Vigée Le Brun gives a vivid description of Staël that aptly complements her painted portrait of the famous writer and that underscores Staël's graciousness as a hostess and her talent as a brilliant conversationalist and especially as an extemporaneous speaker of genius. When moved by inspiration she would express her thoughts with such passion and animation that no one would think of interrupting her. During those moments she impressed her entranced guests as capable of the same poetic improvisations that marked the lyrical flights of fancy of her fictional heroine Corinne.

When Vigée Le Brun's yearning to see Switzerland was fully gratified, she returned to France in 1808 with the firm intention of dividing her time between her house in Paris and a country home she acquired in Louveciennes, which has since become famous for its connection to the Impressionist painters. There she felt she had found a kind of promised land, a place of peace and tranquillity in which to spend the remaining years of her life. She now needed a calm, fairly secluded life away from the upheavals that had buffeted her ever since she had embarked on a career as an artist. Painting, working in her garden, taking long, solitary walks, and entertaining a few close friends on Sundays were her favorite occupations (II, 216). But she had not entirely renounced the artistic and cultural stimulation afforded by the French capital, and her Paris salon became a meeting place of old literary and artistic friends, whose ranks were rapidly being depleted by old age and death. It remained on the periphery of the great new Romantic movements and artists that were beginning to make their mark on the European scene.

Vigée Le Brun experienced a personal loss when, on August 7, 1813, Jean-Baptiste-Pierre Le Brun died. In spite of their divorce in 1794, dictated mainly by political circumstances, they had shared the same house since her return from exile mainly for the sake of convenience, for they had long been personally estranged and she had bitterly resented his infidelities and profligate ways through the years. Yet, she was, as she puts it in *Souvenirs*, "painfully affected by his death" (II, 223). As a knowledgeable and influential art dealer he had facilitated her own career as an artist, and during the Revolution he had staunchly defended her against all the calumnies hurled at her. But the Revolution had ruined his business, and his death left his family with heavy financial obligations and debts.

Political events unexpectedly intervened once more in Vigée Le

Brun's life. After Napoleon's Grand Army disastrous retreat from Russia, the allied armies invaded France and on March 31, 1814, entered Paris.[7] On the night of the same date, Vigée Le Brun had just retired when she was alerted that the Prussians were pillaging and burning the houses and church in Louveciennes. At eleven o'clock her Swiss manservant, who spoke German, entered her bedroom, followed by three Prussian soldiers, their sabers drawn, who promptly proceeded to steal anything of value in the house (II, 205). As soon as the Prussians left, the traumatized Vigée Le Brun was eager to leave Louveciennes and return to Paris.

On April 2, 1814, the Senate decided that Napoleon should be deposed, and on April 6 he was forced to abdicate at Fontainebleau, and the throne was offered to Louis XVIII, brother of the ill-fated Louis XVI, known as comte de Provence, who had fled from the Revolution and spent the years of his exile on the continent and in England. On May 3 the Bourbon dynasty was restored and Louis XVIII entered Paris. On the following day, Napoleon was exiled to the island of Elba.

With Napoleon's abdication Vigée Le Brun began to hope for a return of the Bourbon monarchy. Therefore, on April 12, 1814, she greeted the entry in Paris of comte d'Artois, the younger brother of the future Louis XVIII, with tears of joy and happiness, and she genuinely believed that the majority of the French population shared her enthusiasm (II, 207). She was not entirely wrong in that belief, for by then the disaster of Napoleon's Russian campaign had not only decimated his famed *Grande Armée* and reinforced the European coalition in a stance against him, but even in France public opinion was no longer solidly behind him. Through the festively decorated streets of the French capital and applauding crowds, the Count Artois proceeded to the cathedral of Notre Dame, where a *Te Deum* was celebrated.

When Louis XVIII himself entered Paris, on May 3, 1814, thereby officially consecrating the restoration of the Bourbon dynasty, she rushed to see him in his open carriage among crowds shouting "Vive le roi!" That same evening, there was a festive gathering at the Tuileries Palace, and the king appeared on the balcony to greet the people. As she was eager to see him close up, she lined up with the crowd on the following Sunday as he went to Mass: "As soon as he caught sight of me, he came up to me, gave me his hand in the friendliest manner, and said many flattering things about his pleasure of meeting me" (II, 208). Her great painting of Marie-Antoinette and her children was once more hung on the walls of Versailles. But her elation would not last long.

The new constitution, which strongly favored the upper French classes that were well disposed toward the restoration of the Bourbons, and which deprived the common people of any political influence, did not fare well, either politically or economically, and Louis XVIII eventually failed to gain the support of the majority of the French people. After all, he had returned without their being consulted. General dissatisfaction and even anger grew. Napoleon, for his part, had never resigned himself to his exile to Elba. On March 1, 1815, he landed at Fréjus, near Cannes, with a handful of followers, which grew to thousands in the course of a triumphant march northward toward Paris.[8] Opposition melted away wherever he appeared, for his magnetic personality still strongly appealed to veterans of the Imperial Army and to many French still harboring revolutionary sentiments reinforced by the ferociously repressive measures against all those viewed as enemies of the Restoration, known as the White Terror of 1815, which Stendhal, in his autobiographical *Life of Henry Brulard*, deemed far worse than Robespierre's Terror.[9]

As a staunch monarchist Vigée Le Brun had only favorable things to report about Louis XVIII. She depicts him as a highly cultured person conversant in Latin, eager to protect the arts and letters, lover of the French theater, regular frequenter of the Comédie Française, and great admirer of the actor François-Joseph Talma (II, 211). His favorite pastime was to discuss literature with scholars. In his youth he had himself written poetry, and he had a prodigious memory that enabled him to recite by heart whole stretches of a book, play, or poetry he had read only once (II, 211).

For her part, Vigée Le Brun accurately reports in *Souvenirs* that Louis XVIII and his family left Paris at midnight on March 19, 1815, and that Napoleon entered the French capital the next day. But her interpretation of this historical event understandably reflects her own bias. She was convinced that "he was brought back by the army, supported by bayonets," that "everyone knew all too well that he was bringing back war and ruin to France," and that when he entered Paris he regained possession of the Tuileries at dusk surrounded by his loyal troops but was greeted by a sparse and generally unenthusiastic crowd (II, 209). A more revealing remark is that "the French people are tired of these eternal wars" (II, 210).

During the so-called Hundred Days Napoleon was once more, if only briefly, master of France, and the spirit of the Revolution seemed to be rekindled. He raised a new conscript army with which he marched into Belgium, where the Prussians under Blucher, the English under Wellington, and a mixed force of Belgians and Dutch were ready to oppose him. The Battle of Waterloo, on June 18, 1815, sealed Napoleon's fate, and he would be sent on his final exile on the mid-Atlantic island of St. Helena, where he died on May 5, 1821.

CHAPTER FOURTEEN

$\approx$ *An Active Old Age* $\approx$

SOON AFTER WATERLOO and the 1815 Restoration Vigée Le Brun experienced a cruel personal loss. In early December 1819 she learned that her daughter, Julie Nigris, was ailing and hastened to her side at her Paris apartment on 39, rue de Sèvres. Mother and daughter had long had a difficult, tense relationship, due principally to Julie's headstrong ways, and especially to her ill-advised and ill-fated marriage to Nigris. But they had occasionally seen each other in Paris after Julie's separation from her husband, although Julie stubbornly rejected her mother's repeated offers to come and live with her. But all resentments were instantly forgotten when Vigée Le Brun saw the pretty features of her daughter distorted by physical suffering, a shocking sight that even caused her to swoon (II, 223). Julie's malady, probably pneumonia, progressed very rapidly, and she died on December 8, 1819, leaving a heavy inventory of personal debts, for she had recently been living in straitened circumstances after the return of her husband to Russia and the breakup of their marriage.

Vigée Le Brun's sorrow at losing her only child was immense, and she was haunted by images of the vivacious little girl with large, expressive brown eyes that she had delighted to paint, tenderly nestled in her arms in compositions extolling the joy and sweetness of motherhood. But in real life motherhood had disappointed her, although she felt she had tried her best to combine the demands of her professional life and her responsibilities toward Julie.

That Julie died so suddenly and prematurely at the age of thirty-nine made her loss all the more difficult to bear for her disconsolate mother: "Alas, she was so young! Should she not have survived me?" (II, 224). Added to Vigée Le Brun's sorrow was a sense of unfulfilled hopes and expectations and perhaps also subconscious remorse at not having attempted more effectively to help her daughter financially in her time of need.

Less than a year later, on August 7, 1820, Vigée Le Brun incurred another great personal loss, that of her brother Etienne Vigée. As a child he had been his mother's favorite. Yet the two siblings were quite close and helped each other in their respective careers. He achieved some renown as a poet and playwright, and his sister generously promoted his career and social advancement and was very pleased with his socially brilliant marriage to Suzanne de Rivière. Yet in spite of his successes under the Old Regime, he sided with the Revolution and even engaged in such "patriotic" activities as writing an *Ode to Liberty* denouncing the monarchy and celebrating the fall of Louis XVI. This did not prevent him from being thrown into prison at the end of 1793, and he was saved from the guillotine only by the fall of Robespierre on 9 of Thermidor (July 27, 1794). Upon learning of her brother's revolutionary activities, Vigée Le Brun was understandably angered, and their relationship could no longer be the same after her return to France.[1] Always an adept opportunist, Etienne Vigée also supported Napoleon, whom he celebrated in high-flown verses, but after Waterloo promptly he welcomed the Restoration and extolled Louis XVIII in equally eloquent poems. He was rewarded with the Legion of Honor, notably the prestigious chair of literature at the Athénée, as a successor to the celebrated François La

Harpe, whose famed and influential course, titled the *Lycée*, extolled seventeenth-century classical literature at the expense of the philosophes and the Age of Enlightenment.[2] Like his sister, Etienne Vigée had the ability, talent, and personal charm to survive and even to thrive during the political upheavals of his time. But whereas she remained fiercely loyal to her first royal patrons and unswervingly steadfast in her political beliefs, he was essentially a careerist who had no scruples in switching allegiances in order to further his personal ambitions. No wonder, therefore, that after Vigée Le Brun's return to France their relationship cooled considerably. In *Souvenirs*, however, there is not the slightest mention of their estrangement, and his death clearly affected her profoundly. She sank into a state of depression and melancholy, so much so that her friends, knowing her curiosity and sense of adventure, counseled traveling as a remedy.

In 1820, at the age of sixty-five, Vigée Le Brun undertook her last trip, and her project was relatively modest, but it produced the expected effect. New sites and the challenges of travel uplifted her spirits. She visited Bordeaux and the Loire valley with its Renaissance châteaux. On her way to Bordeaux she stopped off at Méréville in order to see the estate of the immensely wealthy financier Le Comte Alexandre de Laborde, whose father, the court banker Jean-Joseph Delaborde, executed during the Terror, had originally sponsored some of her most notable paintings, in particular her magnificent portrait of Hubert Robert, the painter who excelled in landscapes featuring romantic ruins, as well as her self-portrait embracing her daughter (now both in the Louvre). She found the park at Méréville particularly enchanting and even surpassing "everything one can see in England" (II, 225). And no wonder. It had been largely designed by Hubert Robert in the Italianate style, with picturesque temples, pavilions, and cascades.

Orléans afforded her the exciting view of an active port with all its large and small vessels coming and going in all directions, a sight she deemed as justifying the trouble of having undertaken the trip in the first place (II, 229). She remained in Bordeaux for a full week in order to explore all its treasures, including its surroundings, bringing along her sketchbook in which to jot down particularly striking impressions along her way: "If I noticed on my way an old tower, I climbed up in order to see it up-close" (II, 231). The castles along the Loire, especially the huge Renaissance château of Chambord, built by Francis I and set in an immense park and forest, delighted her visually and evoked in her imagination romantic stories of this great and gallant king. She wished to sketch, then and there, some of the striking architectural features of the château, but was prevented from doing so by an oppressive summer storm (II, 226).

In Tours she visited the cathedral, the ruins of several old châteaux, as well as the medieval monastery of Marmoutier, which was being dismantled, a sight that provoked her indignation: "An infernal band of iron-workers was destroying all these beautiful things! A Dutch mercantile company wanted to buy the monastery in order to turn it into a factory. . . . Vandals themselves would not have done worse" (II, 227). Her guide turned out to be the director of the Academy of Art of Tours, who also went out of his way to introduce her to his students, a gracious gesture that greatly touched her (II, 227).

Refreshed by this journey, Vigée Le Brun returned to Paris with a renewed taste for life and work. She was now ready to settle down permanently and to resume painting. Upon her return from Switzerland she had purchased in 1809 a country house with a large garden in Louveciennes, an attractive small town situated near Versailles at the edge of the Marly forest with a sweeping view of the Seine River and well-cultivated orchards. The town featured the old medieval Church of Saint Martin—in which visitors could view one of Vigée Le Brun's rare religious compositions, a representation of Sainte Geneviève—as well as several châteaux of the seventeenth and eighteenth centuries, all surrounded by beautiful gardens.

Louveciennes is also where the ill-fated Madame du Barry had her private pavilion built for her by Louis XV and designed by the famous architect Claude-Nicolas Ledoux. This is where Madame du Barry had retired after the death of her royal lover in 1774 and where she was arrested in 1793. That she did not face the guillotine with the unflinching stoicism exhibited by both men and women inspired Charles Baudelaire to write a beautiful sonnet singing her praises for having retained her vulnerable humanity and femininity "in those heroic times."[3] As Madame du Barry's portraitist, Vigée Le Brun had been her guest at Louveciennes, and the town and its surroundings had delighted her. She had always loved the countryside and she now decided to divide her time between her Paris residence in the winter, where she held a weekly salon to entertain old friends as well as members of the new generation, such as Louise Colet, mistress of Gustave Flaubert and admirer of her portraits of Marie-Antoinette and a frequent visitor in the 1830s,[4] and her Louveciennes house in the summer, where her social life was perforce more restricted but where she enjoyed gardening and taking long, solitary walks. By an interesting coincidence, Louveciennes is also where the Impressionist painters would find a congenial place of refuge and artistic inspiration.[5]

Vigée Le Brun was chagrined to see the ranks of her dear friends from her brilliant youthful days decimated by old age and death, notably her early supporters and mentors Jean-Baptiste Greuze and Hubert Robert, who died in 1805 and 1808, respectively. Nevertheless, thanks to her personal charm and undiminished vitality, she managed to attract and retain the loyalty of such acclaimed postrevolutionary artists as Baron François Gérard and Baron Antoine Gros, both students of the neoclassical Jacques-Louis David and early exponents and leaders of the movement toward Romanticism. That she could form friendships with artists strongly marked by the glory and downfall of Napoleon is remarkable. She became especially attached to Gros, and, in spite of their sixteen-year difference in age, a warm relationship developed between the portraitist of Marie-Antoinette and the painter who had depicted a dashingly triumphant Napoleon Bonaparte after his defeat of the Italians at the battle of Arcole (1796, Hermitage Museum, St. Petersburg). Gros was made official war painter by Napoleon, and between 1802 and 1808 he painted some of his best-known works, notably *The Plague at Jaffa* and *The Battle of Eylau* (both at the Louvre). The dramatic and vivid combination of romanticism and realism in the way he treated his subjects and handled color earned him great success. In 1811 he received the commission for the cupola of the Pantheon, an official recognition and vast enterprise over which Vigée Le Brun generously rejoiced (II, 220). He managed to make the transition from the Empire to the Restoration, and from 1814 on he was the official portraitist of Louis XVIII. In the 1820s, however, he attempted unsuccessfully to return to a more neoclassical style, and his reputation steadily declined. When a last attempt at a grand neoclassical composition on a Greek legendary theme, *Hercules and Diomedes*, was poorly received at the 1835 Salon, he committed suicide by throwing himself in the Seine.[6] He influenced such great Romantic artists as Géricault and Delacroix, who greatly admired the manner in which he introduced drama, color, and movement in his compositions.[7]

Vigée Le Brun had come to appreciate especially the human qualities of Gros, and his passionate nature appealed to her. She wryly noted that he was rather taciturn and unresponsive in large, purely social gatherings but was at his best in a small, intimate setting: "There his heart revealed itself freely, and this heart was noble and good" (II, 220). She understandably makes no direct reference to Gros's suicide, which went counter to Catholic orthodoxy and to her own religious beliefs, although she was deeply affected by what she euphemistically refers to as his "violent death" (II, 221).

Vigée Le Brun was no longer eagerly sought after as a fashionable portraitist, but painting was still her exclusive passion, and she concentrated on executing pastels and watercolors, primarily for her own pleasure. But she was also preoccupied with her posthumous legacy and reputation. In 1818, she therefore sold to Louis XVIII for the royal collection her formal and imposing portrait of Marie-Antoinette, also known as *Marie-Antoinette en robe de velours bleu* (now in the Musée National de Versailles, with a replica in the Collection Bronson Trevor), which had remained in her possession since she had painted it in 1788.[8] As for her famous portrait of Marie-Antoinette and her children, painted in 1787, she made sure that it would be publicly exhibited in the new museum at Versailles.[9]

Her health was remarkably good, and, in spite of losing several members of her immediate family, she did not have to face a lonely old age thanks to the stimulating company of her loyal friends and admirers who visited her regularly both in Paris and in Louveciennes, particularly two loving and devoted nieces. Caroline de Rivière, daughter of her brother, Etienne, became a constant companion, and in her "tenderness and care" (II, 231) she found a great source of comfort. Eugénie Le Franc, daughter of Le Brun's brother, for her part was also an affectionate and attentive companion. That she also showed a distinctive talent as a portrait painter delighted her aunt, who endeavored to teach and guide her in this demanding profession. Both nieces rekindled Vigée Le Brun's maternal instinct and enriched her last years by bringing the spark and excitement of youth into her life, for in their presence she felt rejuvenated and able to share their enthusiasms and expectations. Thus surrounded by her two nieces and by a devoted circle of old and new friends, Vigée Le Brun spent the last two decades of her life pleasantly and uneventfully, dividing her time between her Paris salon in the winter and her Louveciennes rustic retreat in the summer months.

The profound social and political changes that took place in France after the fall of Napoleon affected her far less directly and dramatically than the French Revolution. She felt at ease under the Bourbon Restoration and enjoyed the benevolent goodwill of Louis XVIII, whom she greatly admired not only for the "courage and sang-froid" (II, 211) with which he dealt with difficult circumstances but more especially for his love of literature, the arts, and, particularly, the theater. She found it noteworthy that the king was a fan of François-Joseph Talma, the leading actor of the day who had also been a favorite of Napoleon, and the two would have lengthy conversations in English in the actor's loge (II, 212).

When Louis XVIII died in 1824, he was succeeded by his brother Charles X, who had left France at the outbreak of the French Revolution and had stayed in England until the Bourbon Restoration. Upon his accession to the throne, Charles X sought to reestablish prerevolutionary privileges for the aristocracy and the clergy, and there was rigid control of the press. Charles X was the embodiment of the party of *ultras*, monarchists who had learned nothing from the French Revolution. Unsurprisingly, Vigée Le Brun could see only his positive side; in *Souvenirs* she lavishly praised his support of artists and related an anecdote illustrating the interest he took in their well-being. On a day he was distributing medals and distinctions to painters and sculptors he caught sight of Vigée Le Brun in the crowd, came over to her, and "expressed so forcefully his joy at seeing me in good health that I was unable to repress my tears of gratitude" (II, 212).

Vigée Le Brun was sixty-five years of age when the 1830 Revolution broke out. Having been on excellent terms with the Bourbons, whom she viewed as kindly and well-meaning, she wondered why "so much virtue and goodness" had not sufficed to avert the July Revolution (II, 213). But she had no personal relationship or kinship with the "citizen king," Louis-Philippe, who was brought to the throne after the July Revolution, thanks largely to the support of the bourgeoisie and the liberal press. Son of Philippe d'Orléans—who was known as Philippe Egalité and who as a Revolutionist had voted for the execution of Louis XVI but had himself ended up on the guillotine in 1793—Louis-Philippe had also emigrated but had refrained from siding with the *ultras*.

The Restoration had been a doomed enterprise in a country that had undergone profound political and social changes. It was an abortive effort at a compromise between the Old Regime, aristocratic in spirit, and the new middle-class society that had benefited from the Revolution. The bourgeoisie, the liberal press, and the people had joined forces in overthrowing Charles X. That for three days—July 27, 28, and 29 of 1830—the French capital was covered with barricades had no apparent impact on Vigée Le Brun.

The increasingly keen awareness of her own mortality greatly preoccupied Vigée Le Brun during those years, and she became obsessed with the idea that she should herself play a direct role in influencing the eventual judgment of posterity on her merits as an artist and on her character as a human being. She was all the more intent on pleading her case for future generations since she had been maligned throughout her career as a woman artist and especially as the official portraitist and protégée of Marie-Antoinette. As a woman who had achieved European renown she could not but be acutely aware that she challenged the traditional notion of womanhood as one of dependence and vulnerability. Her autobiography, modestly and unpretentiously titled *Souvenirs*, relates the successes and hardships of her remarkably long life and prolific career in a vivid and highly personal narrative. The first volume of *Souvenirs* appeared in 1835, and the next two in 1837.

Souvenirs is partly written in epistolary form, for it begins with twelve lengthy letters addressed to Princess Kurakin, sister-in-law of Prince Alexander Kurakin, Russian ambassador in France under Napoleon, whom Vigée Le Brun had met in Saint Petersburg. These letters are followed by thirty-two chapters in a nonepistolary narrative. Then the epistolary form is resumed with nine letters addressed to Countess Vincent Potocka, née Hélène Massalska, a Polish princess who in 1779 had married Charles de Ligne, the son of the famous Prince Charles-Joseph de Ligne, and who after the death of her husband in 1792 had married into Poland's distinguished Potocka family. Then Vigée Le Brun reverts to straight narrative for three more chapters. *Souvenirs* concludes with a series of lively, witty reminiscences titled "Pen Portraits" ("Portraits à la plume") of some of the most notable personalities in society, politics, and the arts she had encountered in a lifetime spanning the Old Regime, the Revolution, the Empire, the Restoration, and the July Monarchy: notably Voltaire, Benjamin Franklin, Talleyrand, Lafayette, Buffon, Delille, Chamfort, Mesmer, Rivarol, David, Robert, Madame de Genlis, and Madame d'Houdetot. The last is evoked in terms that give an idea of the sprightly tone of these delightful "Pen Portraits": "I knew that she was not pretty, but on the basis of the passion she had inspired in J.-J. Rousseau, I thought at least that she would have a pleasant face. . . . She squinted so badly that it was impossible, when she spoke to you, to guess if her words were directed to you. . . . It should nevertheless be said that her engaging mind could make one forget her ugliness. Madame d'Houdetot was kind, generous, cherished with good reason by all those who knew her, and, as I have always found her worthy of inspiring the tenderest sentiments, I have ended up believing, after all, that she could inspire love" (II, 270–1).

Vigée Le Brun attended the apotheosis of Voltaire, which took place at the Comédie-Française on March 30, 1778, after a performance of his play *Irène;* his bust was placed on the stage, and when he appeared in the theatre he was greeted with thunderous and prolonged applause.

Vigée Le Brun gives an account of this famous event and notes that "when a laurel wreath was placed on his head, the illustrious old man appeared so thin, so fragile-looking that I feared this emotional scene would undo him" (II, 343).

Vigée Le Brun saw Benjamin Franklin on numerous occasions during his heyday in Paris in 1778, where he did much to gain French recognition of the American cause. "No one in Paris was more popular, more sought after than doctor Franklin; crowds ran after him in promenades and public places; hats, canes, snuff-boxes, everything was in the *Franklin* style, and one considered it a stroke of good luck to be invited to a dinner that was also attended by this celebrity" (II, 273).

Two artists figure prominently in Vigée Le Brun's "Pen Portraits": Hubert Robert, who had specialized in picturesque landscapes adorned with ancient ruins, and Jacques-Louis David, who had dominated European painting through the Revolution and the Empire. Robert had been one of young Vigée Le Brun's staunchest supporters, and one of her most inspired portraits is that of this artist, executed in 1788 (see plate 2). In sketching his life and career she is understandably sympathetically inclined and stresses his exceptional facility of execution as an artist, his erudition unencumbered by pedantry, his athletic prowess, and his cheerful temperament, which made him "the most amiable person one could frequent in society" (II, 308). Her pen portrait of David, on the other hand, reflects their profound ideological divide, yet acknowledges the fact that he briefly frequented her salon before the Revolution and praised her as an artist even after she fled from France (II, 249). Her main resentment against David was his general behavior during the Terror, and especially his denouncing of artists as political "suspects." Such was the case of Hubert Robert, who was incarcerated and "treated in prison with a harshness bordering on barbarity" (II, 250). No wonder, therefore, that when he let it be known that he greatly wished to meet with her upon her return to France, she left his message unanswered, for she could not bring herself to face the artist who embodied all the revolutionary values she abhorred (II, 250).

Vigée Le Brun's last years were generally untroubled by the tumultuous political events and profound social events shaping modern France and Europe. She was approaching her eighty-seventh birthday—April 16, 1842—when, in the late evening of March 29, she had a few friends for dinner in her Paris residence. After they left, she went to bed and never awakened.

In her will Vigée Le Brun had stipulated that she be buried in the cemetery of Louveciennes, with the simple inscription on her tombstone reading: "Here I rest at last: Louise Elisabeth Vigée Le Brun. Died 30 March 1842. De profundis." Also in accordance with her instructions, the tombstone is adorned with a small medallion showing a laurel wreath surrounding a pedestal on which rest a palette and paintbrushes, the symbols of her life's work.

The rustic setting of Vigée Le Brun's final resting place is not only in keeping with her love of nature. Its geographic proximity to Versailles and its own rich historic past contrast with its unassumingly rural character. Thus it is paradoxically fitting that the remains of the celebrated portraitist of Marie-Antoinette should repose among those of obscure farmers and inhabitants of Louveciennes, a place for which the aging artist had conceived a strong personal predilection.

It might have also pleased Vigée Le Brun to have known that her choice of Louveciennes as a personal refuge where she found peace and comfort in her final years, and where she was also buried, eventually became an integral part of the Impressionist movement. After all, she had always passionately believed in the coloristic values of painting and the sheer visual delight that it should afford the onlooker. In this respect, at least, such artists as Pissarro, Sisley, and Monet, who dwelled and worked in Louveciennes, may have more in common than could be expected with Marie-Antoinette's most talented portraitist.

~ *Afterword* ~

ELISABETH VIGÉE LE BRUN presents the unique case of a great woman artist who consistently subscribed to all the political, social, and religious values of Old Regime France, yet was a revolutionary in the way she fearlessly pursued an independent career as a self-taught, self-supporting painter and as an exile wandering on her own in a Europe torn by revolution and war. She managed, after fleeing from Paris in 1789, to continue painting and setting up studios in Rome, Naples, Venice, Milan, Vienna, Saint Petersburg, and London. Against all odds, she doggedly pursued her calling as an artist and was supremely adept at hiding her fierce determination and dedication as an artist behind a pleasingly gracious persona.

She was a tough fighter and survivor passionately dedicated to her calling as an artist, but also a personal charmer and shrewd self-promoter who early in her career was able to befriend Marie-Antoinette and become her official portraitist, and in the subsequent years gain the confidence and trust of members of the highest European nobility, who willingly sat for her portraits and rewarded her with generous fees. But she was far from a court portraitist merely intent on representing pleasing likenesses of her subjects. She also had a lively mind and a great curiosity about what was going on in the world of arts and letters, hence her warm personal relationship with some of the leading poets and artists of her time.

During Vigée Le Brun's lifetime no French museum exhibited any of her paintings. After her death her niece, Eugénie Le Franc, donated to the Louvre two portraits she had inherited, notably the 1789 *Portrait of the Artist with Her Daughter*. Throughout the Age of Revolution and the reign of Napoleon her 1787 magnificent portrait of Marie-Antoinette surrounded by her children was relegated to a dark corner of the Versailles Palace, but with the Restoration it was proudly reexhibited and is now part of the Versailles permanent collection. Overcoming all odds, Vigée Le Brun has finally had the last word and gained her passport to immortality, for her paintings now hang in all the leading art museums of the world.

NOTES

Introduction

1. Ann Sutherland Harris and Linda Nochlin, *Women Artists: 1550–1950* (New York: Alfred Knopf, 1984), 191. Harris and Nochlin also point out that the Vigée Le Brun oeuvre "has yet to receive the serious treatment it deserves, despite all the fanfare surrounding her career" (190).

2. Germaine Greer, *The Obstacle Race: The Fortunes of Women Painters and Their Work* (New York: Farrar, Straus and Giroux, 1979), 81.

3. Joseph Baillio is putting together the first catalogue raisonné of Vigée Le Brun's prolific but widely dispersed oeuvre. See Joseph Baillio, *Elisabeth Louise Vigée Le Brun* (Fort Worth: Kimbell Art Museum, 1982).

4. Edgar Munhall, "Master Woman Painter in Retrospect," *The New York Times*, Arts Section, August 15, 1982, 23.

5. Michael Levey, *Rococo to Revolution* (New York: Oxford University Press, 1966), 154.

6. Simone de Beauvoir, *The Second Sex*, trans. H. M. Parshley (New York: Vintage Books, 1974), 786.

7. Wendy Wasserstein, "Portraits by a Lady," *Art and Antiques* (September 1989): 109, 129–30. Two fairly recent studies in English deserve mention: Mary Sheriff's highly theoretical and ideological interpretation, *Exceptional Woman: Elisabeth Vigée Le Brun and the Cultural Politics of Art* (Chicago: University of Chicago Press, 1996), and Angelica Goodden's more straightforward narrative, *The Sweetness of Life: A Biography of Elisabeth Louise Vigée Le Brun* (London: Andre Deutsch, 1997).

8. Samia I. Spencer, ed., *French Women and the Age of Enlightenment* (Bloomington: Indiana University Press, 1984), especially "The Novelists and Their Fictions," by Joan H. Stewart, 197–211, "The Memorialists," by Susan R. Kinsey, 212–25, "The Epistolières," by Judith Curtis, 226–41, and "Rousseau's Antifeminism Reconsidered," by Gita May, 309–17.

9. All references to Vigée Le Brun's autobiography are to *Souvenirs,* 2 vols., ed. Claudine Hermann (Paris: Edition des Femmes, 1984). The translations are my own, and heretofore all references to the *Souvenirs* are incorporated in the main text.

Chapter 1. Early Years

1. Denis Diderot, *Salons,* ed. Jean Seznec and Jean Adhémar (Oxford: The Clarendon Press, 1960), II, 3.

2. Elise Goodman, *The Portraits of Madame de Pompadour: Celebrating the Femme Savante* (Berkeley: The University of California Press, 2000). Also see Edgar Munhall, *Greuze the Draftsman* (New York: Merrell in association with the Frick Collection, 2002).

3. Philippe Ariès, *Centuries of Childhood: A Social History of Family Life,* trans. Robert Baldick (New York: Vintage Books, 1962), and Jean-Louis Flandrin, *Families in Former Times,* trans. Richard Southern (Cambridge: Cambridge University Press, 1992).

4. Anita Brookner, *Greuze: The Rise and Fall of an Eighteenth-Century Phenomenon* (London: Elek, 1972). Also Edgar Munhall, *Greuze the Draftsman* (New York: Merrell in association with the Frick Collection, 2002).

5. *Hubert Robert: The Pleasure of Ruins* (New York: Wildenstein, 1988), 11.

Chapter 2. First Successes

1. Joseph Baillio, *Elisabeth Vigée Le Brun* (Fort Worth: Kimbell Art Museum, 1982), 32.
2. Ibid., 60.
3. Ibid., 33.
4. See Michael Fried, *Absorption and Theatricality; Painting and Beholder in The Age of Diderot* (Berkeley: University of California Press), 1980.

Chapter 3. Marriage

1. For more information about the important role salons played in eighteenth-century cultural life, see Dena Goodman, "Enlightenment Salons: The Convergence

of Female and Philosophic Ambition," *Eighteenth-Century Studies* 22, no. 3 (Spring 1989): 329–67; Gita May, "Salons littéraires. France/XVIIIe siècle," in *Dictionnaire universel des littératures* (Paris: Presses Universitaires de France, 1994), III, 3375–77; and Carla Hesse, *The Other Enlightenment: How French Women Became Modern* (Princeton: Princeton University Press, 2001).

2. See Georges May, *Le Dilemme du roman au dix-huitième siècle* (Paris: Presses Universitaires de France, and New Haven: Yale University Press, 1963).

3. See Denis Diderot, *Le Neveu de Rameau* (Paris: Garnier Flammarion, 1963). An excellent English translation was provided by Jacques Barzun and Ralph Bowen, *Diderot: Rameau's Nephew and Other Works* (Garden City, N.Y.: Doubleday and Company, 1956).

4. See Anita Brookner, *Greuze: The Rise and Fall of an Eighteenth-Century Phenomenon* (London: Elek, 1972), and Edgar Munhall, *Greuze the Draftsman* (New York: Merrell in association with the Frick Collection, 2002).

5. See Robert Rosenblum, *Transformations in Late Eighteenth-Century Art* (Princeton: Princeton University Press, 1967), and Hugh Honour, *Neo-Classicism* (New York: Penguin, 1973).

6. For more details about Le Brun's career as an art dealer, see Colin Bailey, *Patriotic Taste: Collecting Modern Art in Pre-Revolutionary Paris* (New Haven: Yale University Press, 2002), 17–18, 185–87, 231–32.

7. See Jean-Louis Flandrin, *Families in Former Times*, trans. Richard Southern (Cambridge: Cambridge University Press, 1992).

8. For more information about Benoist, see Ann Sutherland Harris and Linda Nochlin, *Women Artists: 1550–1950* (New York: Alfred Knopf, 1984).

9. For Rousseau's impact on women of the revolutionary generation, see Gita May, *Madame Roland and the Age of Revolution* (New York: Columbia University Press, 1970); Mary Trouille, *Sexual Politics in the Enlightenment: Women Writers Read Rousseau* (New York: State University of New York, 1997); Madelyn Gutwirth, *Twilight of the Goddesses: Women and Representation in the French Revolutionary Era* (New Brunswick, N.J.: Rutgers University Press, 1992).

10. See Baillio, *Elisabeth Vigée Le Brun*, 134.

Chapter 4. Marie-Antoinette's Portraitist

1. See Chantal Thomas, *La Reine scélérate* (Paris: Seuil, 1989). Translated by Julie Rose as *The Wicked Queen; The Origins of the Myth of Marie-Antoinette* (New York: Zone, 2001). Also see Antonia Fraser, *Marie-Antoinette* (London: Weidenfeld and Nicolson, 2001), and Madelyn Gutwirth, *Twilight of the Goddesses: Women and Representation in the French Revolutionary Era* (New Brunswick, N.J.: Rutgers University Press, 1992), 145–49.

2. In her recent biography *Marie-Antoinette,* Fraser also stresses these kindly traits of the queen, long overlooked by historians and biographers.

3. See Charles-Joseph de Ligne, *Coup d'Oeil at Beloeil,* trans. and ed. Basil Guy (Berkeley: University of California Press, 1991). Also see "Charles-Joseph de Ligne," in Marc Fumaroli, *Quand l'Europe parlait français* (Paris: Editions de Fallois, 2001), 421–30.

4. See Christopher White, *Peter Paul Rubens, Man and Artist* (New Haven: Yale University Press, 1987).

5. See Denis Diderot, *Diderot on Art,* trans. John Goodman (New Haven: Yale University Press, 1995), 2 vols.

6. See *National Museum of Women in the Arts* (New York: Harry N. Abrams, 1987), 34.

7. See Colin B. Bailey, *Patriotic Taste; Collecting Modern Art in Pre-Revolutionary Paris* (New Haven: Yale University Press, 2002), 174.

8. See Simon Schama, *Citizens: A Chronicle of the French Revolution* (New York: Vintage Books, 1989), 227–38.

9. One of Ménageot's best-known compositions, *Leonardo da Vinci Dying in the Arms of Francis the First* (today in the Town Hall of Amboise), was harshly criticized by Diderot in his *Salon* of 1781. See Diderot, *Salons* (Paris: Hermann, 1995), IV, 334–35.

10. For more information about Labille-Guiard, see *National Museum of Women in the Arts,* 33.

11. His composition *The Sabine Women Interrupting the Combat Between the Romans and the Sabines* (today at the Museum of Angers) is considered one of the principal sources of inspiration of Jacques-Louis David's famous *Intervention of the Sabine Women* (Paris, Musée National du Louvre).

Chapter 5. Vigée Le Brun Salonnière

1. See Gita May, "A Courtly Salon on the Eve of the French Revolution," in *Women Writers in Pre-Revolutionary France: Strategies of Emancipation*, ed. C. H. Winn and D. Kuizinga (New York: Garland Press, 1997), 155–62. Also see Colin Bailey, *Patriotic Taste: Collecting Modern Art in Pre-Revolutionary Paris* (New Haven: Yale University Press, 2002), 178.

2. For more information on pre-Romantic pastoral poetry, see Edouard Guitton, *Jacques Delille et le poème de la nature en France de 1750 à 1820* (Paris: Librairie C. Klincksieck, 1974).

3. Denis Diderot, *Salons* (Paris: Hermann, 1984–95), 4 vols.

4. Even Chateaubriand refers to Vigée Le Brun's Greek supper in Book IV of his *Mémoires d'outre-tombe* (*Memoirs From Beyond the Tomb*), ed. Maurice Levaillant and Georges Moulinier (Paris: Gallimard, 1983), 2 vols. Also see George D. Painter, *Chateaubriand* (New York: Alfred A. Knopf, 1978), I, 95.

5. See Chantal Thomas, *La Reine scélérate* (Paris: Seuil, 1989). Translated by Julie Rose as *The Wicked Queen; The Origins of the Myth of Marie-Antoinette* (New York: Zone, 2001). Also see Antonia Fraser, *Marie-Antoinette* (London: Weidenfeld and Nicolson, 2001).

6. For an overview of eighteenth-century art see Michael Levey, *Painting and Sculpture in France, 1700–1789* (New Haven: Yale University Press, 1993).

7. See Dena Goodman, "Enlightenment Salons: The Convergence of Female and Philosophic Ambition," *Eighteenth-Century Studies* 22, no. 3 (Spring 1989): 329–67.

8. See *Souvenirs:* "The first visit I received on the morrow of my arrival was that of Greuze, whom I found unchanged" (II, 102).

9. See Gita May, "A Woman Artist's Legacy: The Autobiography of Elisabeth Vigée Le Brun," in *Eighteenth-Century Women and the Arts*, ed. F. M. Keener and S. E. Lorsch (New York: Greenwood Press, 1988), 225–35.

10. See Fraser, *Marie-Antoinette*, 163.

11. Denis Diderot, *Salon de 1769*, and especially *Salon de 1765* (Paris: Hermann, 1984), 193–96. Also see John Goodman, trans., *Diderot on Art* (New Haven: Yale University Press, 1995), I, 106. For an in-depth analysis of Vigée Le

Brun's portrait of Marie-Antoinette and her children, see Joseph Baillio's two-part article, "Marie-Antoinette et ses enfants par Madame Vigée Le Brun," *L'Oeil* 308 (March 1981): 34–41; 310 (May 1981): 52–61, 90–1.

12. See Antonia Fraser, *Marie-Antoinette*, 156. Also see P. R. Ivinski, H. C. Payne, K. C. Galitz, and R. Rand, *Farewell to the Wet Nurse* (Williamstown, MA: Sterling and Francine Clark Art Institute, 1998).

13. See Antonia Fraser, *Marie-Antoinette*, 228–42.

14. See Georges Bernier, *Hubert Robert: The Pleasure of Ruins* (New York: Wildenstein, 1988).

15. Joseph Baillio, *Elisabeth Vigée Le Brun* (Fort Worth: Kimbell Art Museum, 1982), 95.

16. See Chantal Thomas, *The Wicked Queen*, and Béatrice Didier, *La Musique des lumières* (Paris: Presses Universitaires de France, 1985).

Chapter 6. 1789

1. Antonia Fraser, *Marie-Antoinette* (London: Weidenfeld and Nicolson, 2001), 126.

2. A term of contempt applied by aristocrats to the revolutionaries, especially to the radical republicans belonging to the poorer classes of Paris.

3. Simon Schama, *Citizens: A Chronicle of the French Revolution* (New York: Random House, 1990), 436: "From the very beginning, the violence which made the Revolution possible in the first place created exactly the brutal distinctions between Patriots and Enemies, Citizens and Aristocrats, within which there could be no shades of gray." Also see 445: "In the high summer of 1789 it was the murderously festive action of crowd violence—the evident satisfaction the crowd took from stringing up arbitrarily identified malefactors from the *réverbères* (street lamps) and from parading heads on pikes—that most disturbed 'moderates.'"

4. Isser Woloch, *Transformations of the Civic Order, 1789–1820: The New Regime* (New York: W. W. Norton, 1994), 24.

5. Simon Schama, *Citizens*, 456–70.

6. Jules Michelet, *Les Femmes de la Révolution*, ed. Pierre Labracherie and Jean Dumont (Paris: Club du Livre historique, n.d.), 50. For a study that brilliantly

bridges the gap between history and literature and that gives the lion's share to Michelet, see Susan Dunn, *The Deaths of Louis XVI: Regicide and the French Political Imagination* (Princeton: Princeton University Press, 1994).

7. See especially letter 23 of Saint-Preux to Julie, Part I of *La Nouvelle Héloïse*.

8. Edmund Burke, *A Philosophical Enquiry into the Origin of Our Ideas of the Sublime and Beautiful*, ed. J. T. Boulton (New York: Columbia University Press, 1958). See Gita May, "Diderot and Burke: A Study in Aesthetic Affinity," *Publications of the Modern Language Association of America* (December 1960): 527–39. Also see Samuel H. Monk, *The Sublime* (New York: The Modern Language Association of America, 1935), and Marjorie Nicolson, *Mountain Gloom and Mountain Glory; The Development of the Aesthetics of the Infinite* (Ithaca, N.Y.: Cornell University Press, 1959).

Chapter 7. Rome

1. Lawrence Gowing, *Paintings in the Louvre* (New York: Stewart, Tabori and Chang, 1987), 454–55.

2. Jean-Jacques Rousseau, *Confessions: Oeuvres complètes*, ed. Bernard Gagnebin and Marcel Raymond (Paris: Gallimard, 1959), I, 159.

3. "On account of her love for her art she left for Italy in the month of October, 1789. She went to instruct and improve herself." Quoted in Mary Sheriff, *The Exceptional Woman: Elisabeth Vigée Le Brun and the Cultural Politics of Art* (Chicago: University of Chicago Press, 1996), 223.

4. See Dorothy M. Mayer, *Angelica Kauffmann* (Gerrards Cross, Buckinghamshire: Colin Smythe, 1972).

5. Ibid., 68–71, 81–84, 122–56.

6. Germaine Greer, *The Obstacle Race: The Fortunes of Women Painters and Their Work* (New York: Farrar, Straus and Giroux, 1979), 81; Joseph Baillio, *Elisabeth Vigée Le Brun* (Fort Worth: Kimbell Art Museum, 1982), 100–1.

7. For more details about Ménageot's career, see *Diderot et l'art de Boucher à David* (Paris: Editions de la Réunion des Musées nationaux, 1984), 327–30.

8. This view of Raphael as an artist whose personal life was one of excess and debauchery originates in Giorgio Vasari's famous *Lives of the Artists (Le Vite*

de'piu eccellenti pittori, scultori, e architettori), published in 1550 (revised edition in 1568). See Roger Jones and Nicholas Penny, *Raphael* (New Haven: Yale University Press, 1983), 246: "Why he died we do not know. Vasari believed that it was because he 'continued with his amorous pleasures to an inordinate degree.'" Also see Bruno Santi, *Raphael*, trans. Paul Blanchard (Florence: Scala/Riverside, 1991), 75: "Raphael's health deteriorated rapidly, undermined by his relentless activity and by the excesses of his private life . . . Vasari, not without prejudice, compares the unrestrained life of Raphael to the austere and heroic one of Michelangelo."

9. Diderot's work, begun in 1761, was successively revised until 1782, two years before the author's death. The first publication of this work, based on an autograph manuscript (at the Pierpont Morgan Library in New York), was in 1891. Previous publications, notably that of 1821, had been French retranslations from Goethe's German version, *Rameaus Neffe*.

10. See Georges Bernier, *Hubert Robert: The Pleasure of Ruins* (New York: Wildenstein, 1988).

11. Denis Diderot, *Salon de 1767*, ed. E. M. Bukdahl, M. Delon, and A. Lorenceau (Paris: Hermann, 1995), 335 (my translation). Also see Roland Mortier, *La Poétique des ruines en France* (Geneva: Droz), 1974.

Chapter 8. Naples, Venice, Milan

1. See Joseph Baillio, *Elisabeth Vigée Le Brun* (Fort Worth: Kimbell Art Museum, 1982), 85.

2. See Susan Sontag, *The Volcano Lover* (New York: Farrar Straus Giroux, 1992), for a novelized biography of Hamilton.

3. See Johann Winckelmann, *History of Ancient Art*, trans. G. Henry Lodge (1872–73; rpt. New York: F. Ungar, 1968); Jean Seznec, "Herculaneum and Pompeii in French Literature of the Eighteenth Century," *Archaeology* II, 3 (September 1949): 150–58; Mario Praz, *On Neoclassicism*, trans. Angus Davidson (Evanston: Northwestern University Press, 1969).

4. This explains the title of Susan Sontag's book *The Volcano Lover*.

5. See Edmund Burke, *A Philosophical Enquiry into the Origin of Our Ideas of the*

Sublime and Beautiful, ed. J. T. Boulton (New York: Columbia University Press, 1958); Marjorie Hope Nicolson, *Mountain Gloom and Mountain Glory: The Development of the Aesthetics of the Infinite* (Ithaca, N.Y.: Cornell University Press, 1959); Samuel H. Monk, *The Sublime* (New York: The Modern Language Association of America, 1935).

6. At least according to Susan Sontag, *The Volcano Lover*, 23.

7. See Joseph Baillio, *Elisabeth Vigée Le Brun*, 88.

8. *Chronicle of the Cinema*, with a foreword by Gene Siskel (London: Dorling Kindersley, 1995), 320.

9. Ibid.

10. See Baillio, *Elisabeth Vigée Le Brun*, 89.

11. According to Baillio, ibid., 92, the portrait, executed in 1791, was destroyed in 1940.

12. See Rudolf Wittkower, "Genius: Individualism in Art and Artists," in *Dictionary of the History of Ideas* (New York: Scribner's, 1973), II, 293–312.

13. See Roland Mortier, *L'Originalité, une nouvelle catégorie esthétique au siècle des Lumières* (Geneva: Droz, 1982).

14. See Anita Brookner, *Jacques-Louis David* (New York: Thames and Hudson, 1980), 101.

15. Ibid., 69.

16. Ibid., 99.

17. See Ann Sutherland Harris and Linda Nochlin, *Women Artists: 1550–1950* (New York: Alfred Knopf, 1984), 186.

18. Ibid.

19. At the end of her *Souvenirs* Vigée Le Brun lists her overall oeuvre, of course including primarily her portraits, but also her landscape studies (II, 354). Numbering nearly two hundred in number, this list of predominantly watercolors and pastels also includes sketches and studies in oil and pastel of sites she had found noteworthy in the course of her twelve-year exile and many travels throughout Europe. This aspect of her *oeuvre*, including the thirty-eight wonderful pencil and hand-colored sketches in the Saint Petersburg sketchbook dating from her 1785–1801 stay in Russia (National Museum of Women in the Arts, Washington, D.C.), deserves further study.

20. *Souvenirs*, II, 346.

21. See Gita May, "Rousseau's 'Antifeminism' Reconsidered," in *French Women and the Age of Enlightenment*, ed. Samia I. Spencer (Bloomington: Indiana University Press, 1984), 309–17.

22. Today, this collection is held at La Specola. Mary D. Sheriff accords this episode enormous importance and treats it in considerable detail in *The Exceptional Woman: Elisabeth Vigée Le Brun and the Cultural Politics of Art* (Chicago: University of Chicago Press, 1996).

23. See Jane Martineau and Andrew Robison, eds., *The Glory of Venice; Art in the Eighteenth Century* (New Haven: Yale University Press, 1994).

24. Denon was sufficiently impressed with Vigée Le Brun to write a forty-page biography of her, published in 1792.

25. For more information about this remarkable artist, see Germaine Greer, *The Obstacle Race: The Fortunes of Women Painters and Their Work* (New York: Farrar, Straus and Giroux, 1979), 257–59, and Harris and Nochlin, *Women Artists*, 38–39. Also see Giuletta Chelazzi Dini, Alessandro Angelini, and Bernardina Sani, *Sienese Painting: From Duccio to the Birth of the Baroque* (New York: Abrams, 1998), as well as Sani's *Catalogue Raisonné*.

26. For a colorful biography of Vivant Denon, see Philippe Sollers, *Le Cavalier du Louvre* (Paris: Plon, 1995).

27. See *Romanciers du XVIIIe siècle*, ed. Etiemble (Paris: Gallimard, Bibliothèque de la Pléiade, 1965), II. Also see *Romans libertins du XVIIIe siècle*, ed. R. Trousson (Paris, Laffont, 1994).

28. Jean-Jacques Rousseau, *Confessions: Oeuvres complètes*, ed. Bernard Gagnebin and Marcel Raymond (Paris: Gallimard, 1959), VII, I, 315.

29. In 1794 he published a defense of his wife in a brochure titled *Précis historique de la vie de la citoyenne Le Brun, peintre*. See Appendix III of Baillio, *Elisabeth Vigée Le Brun*.

Chapter 9. Vienna

1. Rousseau's *Promenades of a Solitary Walker* had been published in 1782, at the same time as the first part of the *Confessions*, and there is no doubt that Vigée Le Brun read both texts. It is far less certain that she had the opportunity to

read the second part of the *Confessions*, which appeared in the autumn of 1789, when she hastily fled Paris.

2. For a perceptive study of the impact of the public beheading of Louis XVI on the French collective memory, see Susan Dunn, *The Deaths of Louis XVI; Regicide and the French Political Imagination* (Princeton: Princeton University Press, 1994).

3. See Chantal Thomas, *La Reine scélérate* (Paris: Seuil, 1989). Translated by Julie Rose as *The Wicked Queen; The Origins of the Myth of Marie-Antoinette* (New York: Zone, 2001).

4. For more details, see ibid., 126–27.

5. See Gita May, "Rousseau's Antifeminism Reconsidered," in *French Women and the Age of Enlightenment*, ed. Samia I. Spencer (Bloomington: Indiana University Press, 1984), 309–17, and Mary Trouille, *Sexual Politics in the Enlightenment: Women Writers Read Rousseau* (New York: State University of New York, 1997), 163–92.

6. For more information about the life and career of Charles-Joseph de Ligne, see *Coup d'Oeil at Beloeil*, trans. and ed. Basil Guy (Berkeley: University of California Press, 1991).

7. See Peter Gay, *Voltaire's Politics: The Poet as Realist* (New Haven: Yale University Press, 1988), and Leonard Krieger, *Kings and Philosophers, 1689–1789* (New York: W. W. Norton, 1970).

8. When Diderot made the same voyage in 1773, he arrived in Saint Petersburg on October 8 of that year "more dead than alive" and without having taken a bite for four days. See Diderot, *Mémoires pour Catherine II*, ed. Paul Vernière (Paris: Garnier, 1966), 10.

Chapter 10. The Russian Experience

1. The first biographer of Peter the Great was Voltaire. See *Histoire de l'empire sous Pierre le Grand*, translated by M.F.O. Jenkins under the English title of *Russia Under Peter the Great* (Rutherford, N.J.: Fairleigh Dickinson University Press; London, Associated University Presses, 1983).

2. See Colin Eisler, *Paintings in the Hermitage* (New York: Stewart, Tabori and Chang, 1990), 19–20.

3. For further details on Diderot's relations with Catherine II, see Arthur Wilson, *Diderot* (New York: Oxford University Press, 1972), 442–44, 466–67, 512–14, 518–19, 520–21, 546–47, 650–52, 674–77; and, for his stay in Russia, 631–36, and 639–42. Also see P. N. Furbank, *Diderot; A Critical Biography* (New York: Alfred Knopf, 1992), 301–2, 314, 376–85, 387–88, 392–95. For Voltaire's relations with Catherine II, see Theodore Besterman, *Voltaire* (New York: Harcourt, Brace and World, 1969), 429–30, 492–93.

4. For a recent biography of Catherine the Great, see Isabel de Madariaga, *Catherine the Great* (New Haven: Yale University Press, 1990). Also see "The Tsarina," in *An Imperial Collection: Women Artists from the State Hermitage Museum*, ed. Jordana Pomeroy et al. (London: Merrell, in association with the National Museum of Women in the Arts, Washington, D.C., 2003), 11–17.

5. See de Madariaga, *Catherine the Great*, 27.

6. See Christopher Duffy, *The Military Life of Peter the Great* (New York: Atheneum, 1986) and Nancy Mitford, *Frederick the Great* (New York: Harper and Row, 1970), and for Voltaire's complicated relationship with Frederick, see Peter Gay, *Voltaire's Politics: The Poet as Realist* (New Haven: Yale University Press, 1988).

7. See Eisler, *Paintings in the Hermitage*.

8. Ibid., 12.

9. See Joseph Baillio, *Elisabeth Vigée Le Brun* (Fort Worth: Kimbell Art Museum, 1982), 118.

10. See de Madariaga, *Catherine the Great*, 19 and 155, for more information regarding the numerous and various duties serfs performed for their masters. Also see Olga Cragg-Browzin, "Vigée Le Brun et la société russe à la fin du XVIIIe siècle," in *Catherine II et l'Europe*, ed. Anita Davidenkoff (Paris: Institut d'Etudes Slaves, 1997), 27–34.

11. Ibid., 203.

12. Ibid., chapter 16, "Catherine as Woman and Ruler," 203–18.

13. See Ann Sutherland Harris and Linda Nochlin, *Women Artists: 1550–1950* (New York: Alfred Knopf, 1984), 188–89.

14. See Joseph Baillio, *Elisabeth Vigée Le Brun*, 14.

15. Ibid., 119.

16. For more information about Guérin's career, see *French Painting 1774–1830: The Age of Revolution* (Detroit: Detroit Institute of Arts, 1975), 477–81.

17. See Gita May, "A Woman Artist's Legacy: The Autobiography of Elisabeth Vigée Le Brun," in *Eighteenth-Century Women and the Arts*, ed. Frederick M. Keener and Susan E. Lorsch (New York: Greenwood Press, 1988), 225–35.

18. See Susan Dunn, *The Deaths of Louis XVI: Regicide and the French Political Imagination* (Princeton: Princeton University Press, 1994), for an insightful analysis of the myths that the execution of Louis XVI generated on the part of French historians and men of letters from Chateaubriand to Camus.

19. See Simon Schama, *Citizens: A Chronicle of the French Revolution* (New York: Vintage Books, 1989), 836–47.

20. For more historical details about the Napoleonic era, see Georges Lefebvre, *Napoleon: From 18 Brumaire to Tilsit, 1799–1807*, trans. Henry F. Stockhold (New York: Columbia University Press, 1969), and, by the same author, *Napoleon from Tilsit to Waterloo: 1807–1815*, trans. J. E. Anderson (New York: Columbia University Press, 1969).

21. Pomeroy et al., *An Imperial Collection*, 181.

Chapter 11. Homeward Bound

1. See Edmund Burke's influential treatise of 1757, *Philosophical Enquiry into the Origin of Our Ideas of the Sublime and Beautiful*, ed. J. T. Boulton (New York: Columbia University Press, 1958); Immanuel Kant, *Observations on the Feeling of the Beautiful and Sublime*, trans. J. T. Goldthwait (Berkeley: University of California Press, 1960); and Diderot's *Salons,* especially those sections dealing with the landscapes by Hubert Robert.

2. For more information about Krudener, see E. M. Sartori and D. W. Zimmerman, eds., *French Women Writers* (New York: Greenwood Press, 1991), 253–61. For more information about Adélaïde de Souza, see Joan Hinde Stewart, "The Novelists and Their Fictions," in *French Women and the Age of Enlightenment*, ed. Samia I. Spencer (Bloomington: Indiana University Press, 1984), 204–5.

NOTES TO PAGES 155–169

3. See Georges Lefebvre, *Napoleon: From 18 Brumaire to Tilsit, 1799–1807*, trans. Henry F. Stockhold (New York: Columbia University Press, 1969); and Isser Woloch, *The New Regime* (New York: W. W. Norton), 1994.

4. See "Grimm" and "Correspondance Littéraire" in *Dictionnaire de Diderot*, ed. R. Mortier and R. Trousson (Paris: Champion, 1999).

5. See Simon Schama, *Citizens: A Chronicle of the French Revolution* (New York: Vintage Books, 1989), 842–46, for an account of the dramatic events of 9 Thermidor.

6. See Denis Diderot, *Salon de 1765*, ed. E. M. Bukdahl and A. Lorenceau (Paris: Hermann, 1984), 188–92, for lively descriptions of Greuze's portraits of his wife and a nostalgic evocation of Madame Greuze when she was the youthful and lovely Mademoiselle Babuti.

7. For more information about Greuze's career, see Anita Brookner, *Greuze: The Rise and Fall of an Eighteenth-Century Phenomenon* (London: Elek, 1972).

8. See Edgar Munhall, *Greuze the Draftsman* (New York: Merrell in association with the Frick Collection, 2002), 266.

9. Ibid., color plate 96, 267.

10. Georges Bernier, *Hubert Robert: The Pleasure of Ruins* (New York: Wildenstein, 1988), 12.

11. See Anita Brookner, *Jacques-Louis David* (New York: Thames and Hudson, 1980).

12. See Olivier Bernier, *The World in 1800* (New York: John Wiley and Sons, 2000), 23.

Chapter 12. The English Interlude

1. See Olivier Bernier, *The World in 1800* (New York: John Wiley and Sons, 2000), 98.

2. See Josephine Grieder, *Anglomania in France; 1740–1789* (Geneva-Paris: Droz, 1985).

3. See Theodore Besterman, *Voltaire* (New York: Harcourt, Brace and World, 1969), 525.

4. See J. H. Plumb and H. Wheldon, *Royal Heritage: The Story of Britain's Royal Builders and Collectors* (London: British Broadcasting Corporation, 1977); also Francis Henry Taylor, *The Taste of Angels: A History of Art Collecting from Rameses to Napoleon* (Boston: Little, Brown and Company, 1948).

5. See Sir Walter Besant, *London in the Eighteenth Century* (London and New York: Adam and Charles Black and Macmillan, 1903), 446.

6. See Joseph Baillio, *Elizabeth Vigée Le Brun* (Fort Worth: Kimbell Art Museum, 1982), Appendix VI, 139–40.

7. See Plumb and Wheldon, *Royal Heritage*, 198–242.

8. See Alexander Eliot, *Three Hundred Years of American Painting* (New York: Time Incorporated, 1957), 19–20; also Barbara Novak, *American Painting of the Nineteenth Century* (New York: Harper and Row, 1969), 40–41.

9. See John Gage, *J.M.W. Turner* (New Haven: Yale University Press, 1987), 236.

10. See Patrick Noon, ed., *Crossing the Channel: British and French Painting in the Age of Romanticism* (New York: The Metropolitan Museum of Art in association with Tate Publishing, 2003), 56.

11. Ibid., 40.

12. See J. H. Plumb, *England in the Eighteenth Century; 1714–1815* (Baltimore: Johns Hopkins University Press, 1963), 205–6.

Chapter 13. Return to Imperial France

1. See Georges Lefebvre, *Napoleon: From 18 Brumaire to Tilsit, 1799–1807*, trans. Henry F. Stockhold (New York: Columbia University Press, 1969), 185.

2. See Anita Brookner, *Jacques-Louis David* (New York: Thames and Hudson, 1980), 153.

3. See Gita May, *Madame Roland and the Age of Revolution* (New York: Columbia University Press, 1970).

4. See Joan McDonald, *Rousseau and the French Revolution* (London: Athlone, 1965); Carol Blum, *Rousseau and the Republic of Virtue* (Ithaca: Cornell University Press, 1986); and Roger Barny, *Rousseau dans la révolution* (Oxford: The Voltaire Foundation, 1986).

5. See Madelyn Gutwirth, "Madame de Staël, Rousseau and the Woman Question," *Publications of the Modern Language Association of America* 86, 1 (January 1971): 100–9, and her book *Madame de Staël Novelist: The Emergence of the Artist as Woman* (Urbana: University of Illinois Press, 1978).

6. See Gita May, "Diderot misogyne?" in *Vérité et littérature au XVIIIe siècle*, ed. Paul Aron et al. (Paris: Champion, 2001), 193–98.

7. See Georges Lefebvre, *Napoleon: From Tilsit to Waterloo, 1807–1815*, trans. J. E. Anderson (New York: Columbia University Press, 1969).

8. For more information about the first Restoration, Napoleon's return from Elba, and the Hundred Days, see Lefebvre, *Napoleon: From Tilsit to Waterloo*, 358–68.

9. Stendhal, *Vie de Henry Brulard* (Paris: Gallimard, Bibliothèque de la Pléiade, 1961), 100.

Chapter 14. An Active Old Age

1. For more details about Etienne Vigée's life and career, see chapter 2.

2. See Joseph Baillio, *Elisabeth Vigée Le Brun* (Fort Worth: Kimbell Art Museum, 1982), 33.

3. This poetic homage is titled "To Madame du Barry." See Charles Baudelaire, *Oeuvres complètes*, ed. Y.-G. Le Dantec, rev. Cl. Pichois (Paris: Gallimard, Bibliothèque de la Pléiade, 1961), 222.

4. See Maxine G. Cutler, *Evocations of the Eighteenth Century in French Poetry: 1800–1869* (Geneva: Librairie Droz, 1970), 157.

5. See John Rewald's authoritative and by now classic study, *The History of Impressionism* (New York: Simon and Schuster), 1946.

6. For more information about Gérard and Gros, see *French Painting 1774–1830: The Age of Revolution* (Detroit: Detroit Institute of Arts, 1975).

7. Ibid., 466.

8. See Baillio, *Elisabeth Vigée Le Brun*, 78.

9. See chapter 4 for descriptions of these two paintings.

AUTHOR'S NOTE

THE AUTHOR expresses appreciation to the University Seminars at Columbia University for their help in publication. The ideas presented have benefited from discussions in the University Seminar in Eighteenth-Century European Culture.

INDEX

INDEX